"Into the ongoing debate, confusion, and furor that swirls around women's issues in many of our evangelical churches comes a book that directs our focus upon a biblical understanding of the ministry of the church and presents a practical theology of women's ministry in the local church. It is the blended and united voice of a pastor and a leadership woman. This faithful biblical exposition is a call for a kingdom investment; for the biblical equipping of women to serve God's Bride and to mentor rising generations in the joy and call of their design as women in the church."

—JANE PATETE, Women's Ministry Coordinator,
Presbyterian Church in America

"Susan Hunt and Ligon Duncan have given our churches a celebration of the Scriptures' countercultural plan for the roles of women in Christ's Church. *Women's Ministry in the Local Church* is neither a lofty academic text nor a mere how-to manual. Instead, it is a biblically rich reflection of their very thesis—when men and women humbly and joyfully complement each other's God-given roles and gifts, spiritual grace flows for the nurture of His Church. This is a book you will not only read once but will consult again and again."

—PETER LILLBACK, Senior Pastor, Proclamation Presbyterian Church;
president, Westminster Theological Seminary; author,
*The Binding of God; Calvin's Role in the Development of
Covenant Theology; The Practical Calvinist, An Introduction to
the Presbyterian and Reformed Heritage*

"Finally, Ligon Duncan and Susan Hunt have given the church a clear theological framework from which to build an effective women's ministry. With much of today's women's ministry rooted in pragmatism, it is refreshing and necessary for us to have a resource that helps the church move behind the question of 'how' and to the more important question of 'why.' This work will help pastors and women's ministry leaders think through this important aspect of the church with biblical clarity, theological precision, and complementarian conviction. This is a must-read for anyone concerned about ministry to women."

—DR. RANDY STINSON, Executive Director, Council on
Biblical Manhood and Womanhood

"Women in ministry . . . in the evangelical church there is an embarrassing silence or perhaps a silence of embarrassment. Thankfully, Ligon and Susan have broken that silence by developing a biblical illustrative model of ministry. A complementarian approach honors tradition without the idolatry of traditionalism, addresses the dynamics of our age without the arrogance of modernity, but most of all surfaces a biblical model with relevant text and illustration. Again, biblical light removes the darkness of ignorance."

—HARRY REEDER, pastor, Briarwood Presbyterian Church,
Birmingham, Alabama

"The current clash of biblical and secular cultures over gender issues requires that we diligently and earnestly seek biblical answers to the questions asked by men and women seeking a God-honoring foundation and application of ministry principles. This book combines the fruit of Susan Hunt's spadework in searching the Scriptures for God's design for women who want to serve Christ's church with the scholarly and pastoral gifts of Dr. Ligon Duncan whose own journey with women in Christ's church honors the distinctions between men and women, yet recognizes and blesses the most excellent contributions women make to the church."
—D. JAMES KENNEDY, PH.D., Senior Minister,
Coral Ridge Presbyterian Church, Ft. Lauderdale, Florida

"Pastors desperately need books that ground methodology upon theology—this is indeed such a book. Ligon Duncan and Susan Hunt faithfully uphold the truth of Scripture and winsomely affirm the critical importance of women in the church's life and ministry. What sets this book apart is not only the authors' careful thought but their compelling personal examples. The result is a deeply biblical yet intensely practical guide that will greatly benefit not only women, but pastors as well."
—C. J. MAHANEY, Sovereign Grace Ministries

"When I say that this book is intensely practical, I am not implying it is skimpy in terms of its biblical and theological foundations. It is powerful on both fronts. It spells out the connection between the Bible's clear complementarian teaching about gender issues on the one hand and, on the other hand, a vigorous, affirming, and fulfilling role for women's ministry in the church. You'll know from the very first pages that this is about good theory, for sure, but also about good practice."
JOEL BELZ, founder and chairman, *World* magazine

"Susan and Ligon open their hearts and minds, giving godly instruction from the Scriptures and from their own extensive ministry experiences. They model an appropriate covenantal relationship in the Church between men and women as they help us all to be more faithful in our service to Christ and His Church. This book is intended for women in a women's ministry in the church, but it can help women in every area of their lives. It also can help men appreciate and encourage the ministry of women to each other and help men accept and encourage the appropriate and needed ministry of women to men as well."
—ROBERT C. (RIC) CANNADA, JR., chancellor and CEO,
Reformed Theological Seminary

"This book is a must-read for men and women in the church. Leaders should benefit greatly from this clear biblical/theological approach to the concept of church ministry. It is principally sound and practical throughout. It highlights a wholistic approach to ministry in the church that will give good guidance and advice to local leaders in developing their churches' overall strategy and ministry. Ligon Dungan and Susan Hunt have combined their gifts to encourage and instruct today's Christian woman."
—CHARLES DUNAHOO, CE & P Coordinator, PCA

"It is with sincere gratitude and deep pleasure that I commend this latest work by Ligon Duncan and Susan Hunt to a public that so desperately needs the clear-thinking ideas, as well as the passionate heart for true ministry, contained in this work. Their perspective is as refreshing as it is timeless. Undaunted by the feeble critics of biblical gender roles, we have in this practical volume some of the best wisdom from two of our best counselors on these subjects. Ligon Duncan's credentials, insight, scholarship, and faithfulness are well attested. I am glad to count him as a dear friend, counselor, and fellow pastor. He is a man of integrity and consistency, and his writing is always welcome. What may not be as widely known, however, is how well Susan Hunt practices what she preaches; this pastor wants to vouch for that. Beginning with her own mother and extending to her godly daughters and down to her granddaughters, she is a model of apostolic spiritual mothering. Her mentoring of countless women here and throughout the broader church is a consistent encouragement to this pastor, especially when so many other models and ministries in this area miss the mark. I commend this book to every church for its distilled wisdom that shines the way for all who love the Scriptures. I heartily welcome it as a leader of an improved trend on women's ministry, improved in its movement away from worldliness and in its return to the wisdom of our Creator."

—DAVID W. HALL, Senior Minister, Midway Presbyterian Church,
Powder Springs, Georgia; author of *The Genevan Reformation and
the American Founding* and *The Arrogance of the Modern*

"This book is for women and men who love the church of Jesus Christ and long to see God more fully glorified in the lives of its women. In it Susan Hunt and Ligon Duncan offer a fully biblical approach to ministry that inspires and enables women to flourish in reaching the maximum potential of their divine calling and God-given abilities. *Women's Ministry in the Local Church* is a sensible, practical, encouraging guide to what women can and should be doing in their churches and communities."

—PHILIP GRAHAM RYKEN, Senior Minister, Tenth Presbyterian Church,
Philadelphia; Bible teacher on "Every Last Word"; author of
Ryken's Bible Handbook and Preaching the Word commentaries:
Jeremiah and Lamentations; *Exodus*

"Ligon Duncan and Susan Hunt masterfully present a practical theology for a kingdom-oriented women's ministry. In this day and age, we need more courageous visionaries who seek to release women in ministry while honoring the complementarian framework of God's Word. This is a helpful resource for all who wish to join in this pursuit."

—MARY A. KASSIAN, Distinguished Professor of Women's Studies,
Southern Baptist Seminary, Louisville; author, *The Feminist Mistake*

"This fine book has much wisdom, encouragement, help, challenges, and resources on a vital issue for churches today. It is important for all Christians, men as well as women."

—DR. W. ROBERT GODFREY, president, Westminster Seminary California;
author of *Reformation Sketches* and *An Unexpected Journey*

WOMEN'S MINISTRY in the LOCAL CHURCH

J. LIGON DUNCAN
& SUSAN HUNT

CROSSWAY BOOKS

A PUBLISHING MINISTRY OF
GOOD NEWS PUBLISHERS
WHEATON, ILLINOIS

Library of Congress Cataloging-in-Publication Data
Hunt, Susan, 1940–
    Women's ministry in the local church / Susan Hunt, J. Ligon Duncan.
       p. cm.
    ISBN-13: 978-1-58134-750-0
    ISBN-10: 1-58134-750-2 (tpb)
    1. Women in church work. 2. Women in church work—Biblical teaching. 3. Women in church work—Presbyterian Church in America. 4. Presbyterian Church in America—Doctrines. I. Duncan, J. Ligon, 1960– II. Title.
BV4415.H78   2005
253.082—dc22   2005029172

CH		16	15	14	13	12	11	10	09	08	07	06
15	14	13	12	11	10	9	8	7	6	5	4	3	2	1

From Ligon:
To Anne Harley Duncan, my wife,
and
Sarah Kennedy Duncan, my daughter,
with appreciation and love

From Susan:
To Kathryn Ann (Kate) Coley,
our thirteenth grandchild,
with the prayer that this daughter of the church
will become a woman who loves and serves
the Lord God through His church

Contents

Acknowledgments

FROM SUSAN

I love writing this part of a book because I get to introduce my reader friends to some of the friends who live life with me. Introducing one Christian to another Christian is so profound. It is so eternal. After all, one day we will all live life together—forever.

The women who have shown me what it means to serve Christ through His church are too numerous to mention. I do not even know many of their names, but I have seen them in their churches around the world. Their faces and ministries are ever in my heart.

The two women who taught me most about what it takes to lead a women's ministry in a local church are our daughters, Kathryn Barriault and Laurin Coley. Both have served as president of the women's ministry in their respective churches. They taught me about sacrificial servant-hood rooted in love for Christ and His Church.

I wish I could list the name of every woman in Midway Presbyterian Church. They are my teachers, encouragers, and friends. The leaders of the women's ministry, especially the Titus 2 Committee—Ann Kistner, Patsy Kuipers, Denise Monroe, and Sandra Westerfield—gave me confidence to write this book because their ministry shows me that the concepts in this book really do work. The women in the Tuesday Morning Bible Study listened as I taught the Pastoral Letters. Their insights and questions helped shape this book. Their prayers help shape me.

Sharon Betters, Lynn Brookside, Karen Grant, Jane Patete, and Barbara Thompson share and feed my passion for women's ministry. Their heart-prints are all over this book.

The men who teach me are also too numerous to mention, but one stands above them all. My husband, Gene, teaches me much from the pulpit, but it is his life that daily shows me what it means to love the church.

I am grateful to Charles Dunahoo who asked me to serve as Director of the Women In the Church ministry for the Presbyterian Church in America and who patiently taught me how to do what he hired me to do; to David Hall, the Senior Pastor of our church, who encouraged me to write this book and who read and reacted to the chapters; to the elders of our church whose leadership provides a good place for women to serve Christ; and to George Grant whose friendship, lectures, and books help Gene and me think sweeter and stronger thoughts about God.

Countless women join me in thanking Ligon Duncan for his commitment to women's ministry in the church. We have learned from his teaching and rejoiced in his leadership, but working on this project took me to new levels of appreciation. Ligon did not have time to write this book, but he did it anyway because he believed it to be important.

The men and women who wrote supporting testimonies for the chapters in this book made this work stronger. I thank them all.

My thanks to the fine people at Crossway for their courageous commitment to complementarianism and their encouragement to me personally.

Our children and grandchildren contribute to everything I do because they contribute to who I am. Kathryn, Dean, Hunter, Mary Kate, Daniel, Susie, and Sam Barriault; Richie, Shannon, Mac, Angus, and Heather Hunt; and Laurin, Scott, Cassie, Scotty, Maggie, and Kate Coley have "entered into a covenant to seek the LORD, the God of their fathers, with all their heart and with all their soul" (2 Chronicles 15:12). Gene and I "have no greater joy than to hear that [our] children are walking in the truth" (3 John 4).

And thanks to Mama for praying for me and for cooking dinner so I could write. Gene thanks you too.

FROM LIGON

I want to record here my happily acknowledged debt to so many godly Christian women in the local churches I have served over the course of the years. Many of them have been heaven-sent blessings to me, and their character and example have left an indelible impression upon me. The Christian women of the Second Presbyterian Church of Greenville, South Carolina (the church of my youth) taught me in Sunday school and VBS, helped me with the catechisms, and prayed for me for a quarter of a century (and some still do!).

The women of the Covenant Presbyterian Church of St. Louis, Missouri, during my seminary years, as I served as a youth director and intern, were a great encouragement to me. Especially the extraordinary young women in the youth program (their love for the Lord and his Word was so edifying to me), many of whom I have followed with interest as they have become wives and mothers and have served the Lord in various professions. I am so proud of you all.

The ladies of the Trinity Presbyterian Church of Jackson, Mississippi, showed Christian hospitality to me as a young seminary professor and a very "green" assistant pastor. Your contagious zeal for missions set a beautiful example for me and others. The women of the First Presbyterian Church, Yazoo City, Mississippi, where I served for much of 1993 as interim pastor, manifested grace under trial and faith in time of loss that are marked in my heart as standing witness to the trustworthiness of our God in every circumstance of life. Anne and I will not forget your Christian kindness and warmth.

My dear sisters in Christ at the First Presbyterian Church, Jackson, Mississippi, where I have now served for almost a decade, I cannot adequately thank you or give to God enough praise for you. I stand in awe as I contemplate the unique combination of your abilities, energy, dedication, love for the truth, care for your families, and desire to minister to those within and without the church. No pastor could hope for a better flock, and it is a privilege to work with you in training up another generation of godly Christian women, committed to the gospel, the local church, the Great Commission, the Scriptures, and the Bible's teaching on male-female role relationships in home and church.

My dear wife, Anne, is my greatest earthly treasure, and my respect for her grows daily. She is a woman of integrity, intelligence, compassion, and action. I am humbled when I contemplate her character, grateful to God that she is my wife and the mother of my children, and motivated to grow in Christian maturity just because I know her. I love you, Anne, but not as much as you deserve, for you are a woman of great worth.

My daughter, Sarah Kennedy, you are a delight, and I can already see in you the strong traits of Duncan, Ledford, Harley, and Luther women from whom you are descended (what a covenant legacy you have). I can't wait to see what the Lord will do in your life. It is my earnest desire that you will be a "woman who fears the Lord." I love reading the Bible, learning catechism answers, praying, and talking with you.

Lastly, thanks to Susan Hunt, who has so patiently endured my tardiness and every other frustration I have thrown her way during the course of producing this volume. I have admired Susan for a long time, and it has been a privilege to work with her.

Part 1

INTRODUCTION

The purpose of this book is to strengthen Christ's Church by presenting a practical theology of women's ministry in the local church.

The book will answer five fundamental questions:

- Why should a church have a women's ministry—what is the biblical apologetic?

- Who is responsible for the women's ministry in a church?

- How does a women's ministry relate to the other ministries in a church?

- What are the tasks of a women's ministry?

- How does a church implement a biblical approach to women's ministry?

1

The Story

The source and origin of the Church is the free love of God. . . . In the whole world there is nothing enduring but the Church. . . . Her happiness must be considered in consisting principally in this, that she has reserved for her an everlasting state in heaven. . . .

JOHN CALVIN[1]

*T*he subject of this book is not women; it is the Church of the Lord Jesus. Though the focus of the book is one specific area of the church's ministry, a biblical understanding of the church acknowledges that no part stands alone. A women's ministry is one component of the total life and work of a local church.

The authors of this book have had separate journeys to a shared commitment to women's ministry in the local church, but for both of us this commitment is one part of a larger commitment to and love for the household of God. As Dr. Edmund Clowney wrote, "If we lack interest in the church we lack what for Jesus was a consuming passion. Jesus loved the Church and gave himself for it (Eph. 5:25)."[2]

LIGON'S STORY

I was born and reared during a time of tremendous cultural and ecclesiastical transition in the United States relating to the whole complex of issues surrounding manhood and womanhood and male-female role relationships in the home and church. But I was also reared in a Christian family with a godly father and mother who lived out, in the home, church, and community, with no fanfare whatsoever, a beautiful biblical pattern of manhood and womanhood. I have also had and continue to enjoy the privilege of Christian fellowship and mutual ministry with numerous godly, gifted, consecrated, complementarian Christian women. These women have shown me what biblical women's ministry in the local church looks like in action. Thus my own appreciation of the importance of women's ministry in the local church flows out of biblical conviction, is reinforced by church experience, and is heightened by the fact that gender issues are the wedge of a worldview megashift in our own times.

The 1960s brought a cultural revolt against the traditional roles of men and women in our society that spilled over into many mainline churches. One consequence was that these churches abandoned fidelity to the clear biblical teaching requiring godly qualified men to serve as the shepherds-teachers-leaders of the local church. My father was not a pastor, but he was an elder (an eighth-generation elder, to be exact!) in our local church—a part of one of those wavering mainline denominations. He loved his church but wanted to be a part of a denomination with a high view of Scripture and an unwavering commitment to the gospel of our Lord Jesus Christ. One of the obvious ways our denomination had demonstrated its low view of Scripture was the issue of women's ordination to the teaching and ruling office of the church. As a teenage boy in the 1970s, I watched my father, at great personal cost and with many tears, leave the denomination of his youth and young manhood and become a founding father of a family of churches committed to standing with the Bible and against cultural capitulation on gender issues, among many others.

In those days, one of the things that was frequently alleged against the many Christians and churches that comprised this new denomination (the Presbyterian Church in America) was that we were "anti-women," that we oppressed women and did not value them or allow them to use their gifts. This accusation never got the slightest traction with me because I had personally experienced just the opposite. I was reared in the company of godly, smart, educated, theologically sound women who had devoted their lives to the work of the church, who were unreservedly and gladly committed to the Bible's teaching on male-female role relationships, and who were deeply appreciated and respected by the male spiritual leadership of the local church. And I have been surrounded by and delighted in such esteemed sisters in the Lord all my life.

My grandmother was the only one of her many siblings to graduate from college. She put herself through on a basketball scholarship in the midst of a war and depression. She was intelligent and hard-working and devoted herself to the Southern Baptist churches of East Tennessee where she lived. Whether it was choir, Sunday school, Training Union, or VBS, Audrey Mae Ledford was ably serving the Lord and his people. She had not the slightest desire to preach or hold the office of pastor and would have told any woman who did that she was "plumb crazy." She lived out Titus 2:3-5 and spiritually mentored generations of women in Tennessee and Florida.

My mother was a university professor, as well as a lifelong church music director. She started school at the age of three, finished college while still a teenager, did graduate study at the Southern Baptist Theological Seminary in Louisville, Kentucky, and postgraduate work at Northwestern in Chicago, and directed church choirs in Tennessee, North Carolina, Georgia, and South Carolina. After joining the faculty at Furman University, she threw the Athletic Department into a tizzy by flunking half of the baseball team in what they thought was a "crip course" in Music Appreciation. Only my dad's secret intervention in grade curving on their behalf saved the day. Mom was a tough and respected prof—demanding academically and outstanding professionally.

Mother thinks theologically and deeply, writes beautifully, is a gifted public speaker, works harder than anyone I know, and has poured her whole life into the service of Christ and His people. I have had the enormous privilege of fellowship with some of the brightest theological minds in the English-speaking world over the last thirty years (often in my family's home around the dinner table), and Mother is every bit their intellectual peer. Yet she has never aspired to the eldership, nor resented male spiritual leadership. Indeed, she has gloried in it and delighted to support the ministry of a godly succession of pastors and elders in our home church, all the while joyfully embracing the biblical teaching on male-female role relationships. None of the women whom I have known over the years who have aspired to the teaching office of the church, and who are often offended by what they perceive as the church's lack of recognition of their gifts and sense of calling, are her superior—academically, intellectually, or otherwise. But Mother has always disdained recognition. She has always been about service, not status. And she has been a spiritual mother to generations of women within and without her local church.

My wife, Anne, holds two advanced degrees, and before we married she spent more than a decade on the church staffs of two large and vital, capital-city, downtown, evangelical churches. She grew up in a mainline egalitarian church and professed faith in college. She learned her theology on her own at first. Nobody spoon-fed it to her. She embraced complementarianism on purpose. Nobody forced it on her, and she didn't just assume it. Having taught elementary school, and having worked in Christian education in her home church, Anne went on to study with David Wells and a host of his stellar colleagues at Gordon-Conwell Seminary in Massachusetts. Then after years of faithful service in the field of Christian education, and having pursued doctoral course work at Trinity in Chicago, she completed a second Master's degree (in Marriage and Family Therapy) at Reformed Theological Seminary.

Anne worked in Christian Education, youth, singles, missions, and women's ministry. Everything she did, she did well. Once she was given the option of writing her own title and job description, and she chose the title Adult Christian Education Coordinator instead of a more encompassing title, out of the conviction that the role of facilitating the Christian Education of the whole church, men and women, was the role for a pastor or elder, and she wanted it clearly understood that she would be working in support of the leadership and work of a pastor and the elders. The men didn't force this on her. She expected it of them! Anne's life and ministry has had a profound impact on men and women in four local congregations over the course of more than two decades. And she has poured herself into the discipleship of women in the church.

Then there is my friend and colleague Donna Dobbs, Director of Christian Education in the congregation I serve. I have the joy of working with Donna (and our faithful Director of Women's Ministry, Liz

Griffin) in facilitating the discipleship of our women in the church. Donna is as solid as the day is long theologically and firmly complementarian, delights in the leadership of our elders, and is enthusiastic about the educational ministry of the church and committed to cultivating a women's ministry in the local church that complements and supports the work of the pastors, elders, and deacons, that nurtures and equips our women for growth and service, and that promotes a comprehensive biblical view of manhood and womanhood.

What have I learned from these gifted and godly women (and I wish I could tell you more about them, and others)? Well, first, I have seen the impact of their ministry to women multiplied in the women they have discipled as those women take up the torch of service and women's ministry in the local church and of Christian marriage and motherhood in the home. Second, I have seen in them the glorious results of pastors who invested in them, so that they were better equipped to invest in the women they discipled. For instance, I think of the way Gordon K. Reed and Paul Settle, two pastors of my home church (both of them widely respected evangelical leaders), invested in my mother, equipping her to better disciple other women in our church and in the wider Christian community. I reflect on how Glen Knecht and Mark Ross, truly extraordinary ministers, under and with whom my wife worked in Columbia, South Carolina, poured their wisdom, experience, and love for God and his people into Anne as she served with them. She was already wise, and they were God's instruments to make her even wiser, and how that investment has paid off in the lives of countless women and families! Third, I have seen in them a real, tangible, and practical love for the whole church. Their commitment is to a women's ministry that serves the interests of the whole body and results in blessing for the whole congregation. In other words, their approach to women's ministry is not consumer-oriented ("we deserve a ministry that focuses on us"), but kingdom-oriented ("how can we invest in women in a way that equips them as disciples, for their own spiritual maturation, for the good of the marriages and families of the church, for the betterment of the total ministry of the church, and for their life in the world?").

So, in a sense the reason I am coauthoring this book is because of godly women like Audrey Mae Ledford, Shirley Ledford Duncan, Anne

Harley Duncan, Donna Dobbs, Liz Griffin, Susan Hunt, and more. I am the beneficiary of their spiritual maturity and service in the church, but as a shepherd I am also responsible for preparing women in the church like them for service in the church. I want to help encourage and equip women in the local church, and to help those women invest themselves in mentoring a new generation of women to serve in the church. But what this encouragement aims for our Christian women to do, and to what ends, is a vitally important (and disputed) matter today because of widespread confusion, even in evangelical churches.

On the one hand, some church leaders are so afraid of women assuming unbiblical roles in the church that they fail to equip them for the roles to which they have been indisputably called in the home and church. On the other hand, in the name of not squandering women's gifts and abilities, Christian women are often encouraged to take up unbiblical roles in the life of the church, even in Bible-believing congregations. For women's ministry in the local church to do the job of discipleship biblically will require the avoidance of both these errors.

For these reasons and more, I treasure the opportunity to address this subject, especially with a colleague who is a respected author and veteran leader in women's ministry, as well as a faithful wife, mother, and grandmother. It is vital that we get this right, for the sake of the health and witness of the local church.

SUSAN'S STORY

It has taken thirty years for the Lord to prepare me to write this book. My husband and I were in our early thirties when we became part of a new denomination, the Presbyterian Church in America, which was committed to the inerrancy of God's Word. (For information on the doctrinal standards and ecclesiology of the Presbyterian Church in America, visit www.pcanet.org.) We left a church that ordained women to the eldership and became part of a church that held to male headship. It was the 1970s. We were swimming against the theological and cultural current, but we knew it was right.

My involvement with women's ministry initially grew out of my husband's concerns and not my own zeal. He was the pastor of a new church, and the people attending were from a variety of theological backgrounds. Gene quickly realized the need for the church to provide discipleship and ministry opportunities for women that were consistent with our theological standards, integrated with the total life of the church, and under the oversight of the elders. He decided that we needed a weekly women's Bible study, and he wanted me to teach it. I had little passion for this because my ministry zeal was for children, but I agreed with his concern. As I experienced the wisdom of his decision, my passion for women's ministry slowly grew.

When our denomination was formed, the women's ministry was placed as a department of the Christian Education and Publications Committee. Strong foundations and purposes for this ministry were put in place. Fourteen years later, in 1987, the Christian Education Committee made the decision to hire a staff person to give increased direction to women's ministry. It was a timely and strategic decision. I am extremely grateful for the priority the male leadership gave to women's ministry and for the privilege they gave me to serve as director of this ministry. I approached this task with questions:

• What does the Bible say about womanhood?

• I know what women are *not* to do in the church, but what *are* we to do?

• How can the whole range of women's gifts be utilized without compromising male headship?

I was surrounded by a committee of godly women who were also committed to discovering the answers to these questions. We served under the guidance and oversight of the Christian Education Committee, and this ecclesiastical context gave us the safety and security to explore these questions with integrity. From the beginning of our pilgrimage to understand biblical womanhood, there were some non-negotiables:

• The authority of God's Word.

• The theological standards of our denomination.

• The ecclesiastical structure of our denomination.

I find great joy in the fact that we did not have a grand vision and strategy—but then again maybe we had the grandest of visions and strategies because we resolutely believed that our chief end is to glorify God, and that includes our pursuit to understand what Scripture says about womanhood and woman's place in the church. The vision and strategy grew as we studied God's Word.

As we surveyed the church, culture, and available resources, several things emerged:

• There were books that discussed a woman's relationship with Christ, but we could not find a clearly defined and articulated apologetic for biblical womanhood. At the same time, the culture was front and center with an apologetic that was antithetical to biblical truth.

• There were books that explained the theology of male headship, but we could not find books that helped women understand their relationships and responsibilities in God's family.

• The majority of models and resources for women's ministry were parachurch (a separate organization from the church), auxiliary (ministries focused on special projects), or counseling (ministries focused on the needs of individual women). We could not find women's ministry models and resources that were church-integrated and corporate-focused.

We were shocked to realize the silence of the evangelical church on this topic. It was clear that culture, not the church, was setting the agenda for women. We studied, talked, prayed, and wrote. The result is a biblical apologetic for womanhood that is set forth in a series of books and Bible studies for women called *Biblical Foundations for Womanhood* (see Resources below).

But a persistent question keeps popping up in my own mind and is frequently asked by others: Why should a church have a women's ministry?

The question needs a clear and concise answer, and I am delighted to partner with Dr. Ligon Duncan on this project. His credentials are obvious, but there are less obvious factors that are equally important to me. First is his marriage to Anne. My observation is that a pastor's attitude about women in the church is inextricably linked to his marriage. Second, I have been encouraged by conversations with women from the church he pastors as they have spoken of the support and leadership he gives to women's ministry. Third, Ligon represents the current generation of church leaders. His willingness to participate in this project gives me great hope that the work and witness of God's church will not be diminished by accepting the cultural abandonment of gender distinctiveness or by ignoring the worth of suitable helpers.

When I started this journey my husband and I had two young daughters and a son. Now we have seven granddaughters, one of whom has preceded us to heaven, and six grandsons. For theological and personal reasons I am more passionate about God's Church and His design and calling for women in His Church than I was thirty years ago. As I begin this book I am full of gratitude to my Sovereign. He has never left me, and He continually guides me. I know what Dr. Jack Miller meant when he wrote about "the presence of the Father carrying you where your own feet never could."[3]

Once again I embark on a journey where my own feet could never take me.

RESOURCES

This book builds on two bodies of work: The *Danvers Statement on Biblical Manhood and Womanhood* and the *Biblical Foundations for Womanhood* materials.

The Danvers Statement on Biblical Manhood and Womanhood

The "Danvers Statement" has become widely recognized as the best unifying, summary expression of what conservative, Bible-believing evangelical Christians accept as the teaching of Scripture regarding manhood and womanhood. It was drafted by several key evangelical leaders at a meeting in Danvers, Massachusetts, in December 1987 and was first published in final form by the Council on Biblical Manhood and Womanhood (CBMW) in Wheaton, Illinois, in November 1988. It provides a brief rationale for why the church cannot afford to remain undecided or uncommitted on the issue of male-female role relationships in home and church, it sets out the core purposes of the Council on Biblical Manhood and Womanhood—perhaps the major evangelical organization working to promote a robust biblical view of manhood and womanhood in evangelical churches today—and then presents ten affirmations based on the Bible's teaching on manhood and womanhood. The ten affirmations are listed below. See Appendix 1 for the Rationale and Purposes of the "Danvers Statement."

Ten Affirmations

Based on our understanding of Biblical teachings, we affirm the following:

1. Both Adam and Eve were created in God's image, equal before God as persons and distinct in their manhood and womanhood (Gen 1:26-27, 2:18).

2. Distinctions in masculine and feminine roles are ordained by God as part of the created order, and should find an echo in every human heart (Gen 2:18, 21-24; 1 Cor 11:7-9; 1 Tim 2:12-14).

3. Adam's headship in marriage was established by God before the Fall, and was not a result of sin (Gen 2:16-18, 21-24, 3:1-13; 1 Cor 11:7-9).

4. The Fall introduced distortions into the relationships between men and women (Gen 3:1-7, 12, 16).

In the home, the husband's loving, humble headship tends to be replaced by domination or passivity; the wife's intelligent, willing submission tends to be replaced by usurpation or servility.

In the church, sin inclines men toward a worldly love of power or an abdication of spiritual responsibility, and inclines women to resist limitations on their roles or to neglect the use of their gifts in appropriate ministries.

5. The Old Testament, as well as the New Testament, manifests the equally high value and dignity which God attached to the roles of both men and women (Gen 1:26-27, 2:18; Gal 3:28). Both Old and New Testaments also affirm the principle of male headship in the family and in the covenant community (Gen 2:18; Eph 5:21-33; Col 3:18-19; 1 Tim 2:11-15).

6. Redemption in Christ aims at removing the distortions introduced by the curse.

In the family, husbands should forsake harsh or selfish leadership and grow in love and care for their wives; wives should forsake resistance to their husbands' authority and grow in willing, joyful submission to their husbands' leadership (Eph 5:21-33; Col 3:18-19; Tit 2:3-5; 1 Pet 3:1-7).

In the church, redemption in Christ gives men and women an equal share in the blessings of salvation; nevertheless, some governing and teaching roles within the church are restricted to men (Gal 3:28; 1 Cor 11:2-16; 1 Tim 2:11-15).

7. In all of life Christ is the supreme authority and guide for men and women, so that no earthly submission—domestic, religious, or civil—ever implies a mandate to follow a human authority into sin (Dan 3:10-18; Acts 4:19-20, 5:27-29; 1 Pet 3:1-2).

8. In both men and women a heartfelt sense of call to ministry should never be used to set aside biblical criteria for particular ministries (1 Tim 2:11-15, 3:1-13; Tit 1:5-9). Rather, Biblical teaching should remain the authority for testing our subjective discernment of God's will.

9. With half the world's population outside the reach of indigenous evangelism; with countless other lost people in those societies that have heard the gospel; with the stresses and miseries of sickness, malnutrition, homelessness, illiteracy, ignorance, aging, addiction, crime, incarceration, neuroses, and loneliness, no man or woman who feels a passion from God to make His grace known, in word and deed, need ever live without a fulfilling ministry for the glory of Christ and the good of this fallen world (1 Cor 12:7-21).

10. We are convinced that a denial or neglect of these principles will lead to increasingly destructive consequences in our families, our churches and the culture at large.

CBMW has many other resources that will prove helpful to any church leader desirous of inculcating biblical principles on male-female role relationships in the home and church or cultivating an approach to the ministry to and of women in the church that joyfully embraces biblical teaching. Visit www.cbmw.org for more resources.

Biblical Foundations for Womanhood

This series of discipleship materials for women is comprised of two complementary and intersecting tracks. The overarching objective of this curriculum is to equip women to think biblically and live covenantally.

• Track #1: Topical studies that teach biblical principles of womanhood. These include: *Leadership for Women in the Church, Spiritual Mothering, By Design, The True Woman, Treasures of Encouragement,* and *The Legacy of Biblical Womanhood.* There is a Leader's Guide for each book.

• Track #2: Bible studies written specifically for women that use the biblical principles of womanhood to apply Scripture to life. These studies include: *Paul's Letters to Maturing Churches* (Ephesians, Philippians, Colossians, 1 and 2 Thessalonians), *The Formation of God's People Israel* (Exodus), *The Gospel of Matthew Part 1 and 2, The Pastoral Letters* (1 and 2 Timothy and Titus). There is a commentary, Leader's Guide, and student book for each study.

For more information visit www.pcanet.org/cep/wic.

To order, go to www/cepbookstore.com or call 1-800-283-1357.

HOW TO USE THIS BOOK

This book has multiple uses. An individual man or woman may read it to think through issues relating to women's ministry in the church. However, the Leader's Guide for this book provides lesson plans and processes to help church leadership assess the need for a women's ministry, determine a structure for that ministry, and train women for leadership in the women's ministry. The Leader's Guide includes a resource section with articles, practical ideas for events and ministries, and a wealth of other helpful information (available from www.cepbookstore.com or call 1-800-283-1357). The greatest benefit of the book is for church leadership—male and female—to use the book and Leader's Guide to:

• *Study*: the first step in a biblical approach to women's ministry is for church leadership to have a biblical apologetic for women's ministry. The book could be read and discussed by elders, the Christian education committee, or a task force appointed to study women's ministry.

• *Evaluate*: determine strengths and weaknesses of the existing ministry.

• *Reorganize*: determine a focus and direction and ways to implement needed changes.

• *Organize*: plan for a new ministry.

• *Train*: yearly training of leaders will help maintain theological grounding and prevent the ministry from becoming task-driven.

• *Recruit*: give potential leaders a biblical vision for women's ministry by asking them to read the book and then to pray about assuming a position of leadership.

• *Educate*: If a church is beginning a women's ministry, teach it to the women at large, perhaps in a women's Sunday school class, so that women understand a biblical approach to women's ministry. It could also be used in conjunction with the *Biblical Foundations for Womanhood* Bible study on the Pastoral Letters.

Our prayer is that God will be pleased to use this book to help the church "grow up in every way into him who is the head, into Christ, from whom the whole body, joined and held together by every joint with which it is equipped, when each part is working properly, makes the body grow so that it builds itself up in love" (Ephesians 4:15-16).

Dr. Charles H. Dunahoo, Coordinator of Christian Education and Publications for the Presbyterian Church in America, author of MAKING KINGDOM DISCIPLES

When the Presbyterian Church in America was formed, we attempted to develop a denomination that included all phases of the church's life. There were strategic reasons for making an active and viable women's ministry a priority.

First, throughout biblical history and the ongoing life of the Church, women have played a vital role in both Church- and kingdom-related ministries. Godly women have served in important roles in local churches, in denominations, and in world missions, as well as in many types of mercy ministries. Godly women have served faithfully in the Church, along with its officers, to demonstrate the wholeness of God's covenant people. There are numerous biblical examples of such labors.

Second, because the Church "grows and builds itself up in love, as each part does its work" (Ephesians 4:16, NIV), the apostle Paul indicates that each part, or person, in the church should be trained and equipped for ministry, and this includes the women in the church.

Third, our desire was to speak clearly to men and women regarding their roles among God's covenant people and to develop a structure that would allow them the cooperative freedom to fulfill those roles in the Church.

Fourth, the choice was made by the organizing committee of the denomination to position the women's ministry with the Christian Education and Publications Committee because of its assignment to equip people for ministry. Discipleship and ministry have characterized the women's ministry from the beginning.

This kind of emphasis on women's ministry has helped create a spirit of oneness and unity that has forged a unique identity throughout the denomination. Women are involved in the life of the church in significant ways. Women have been and are:

• faithful in prayer.

• helpers in teaching the biblical and theological truths upon which the denomination was founded.

• key people in mercy ministries.

• supporters of the whole work of the church.

Our church standards encourage officers to select godly women to work with them in ministry. While respecting the role of ordained male leaders in their oversight of the church's ministries, including women's ministries, the PCA has an effective and strategic women's ministry at each level of the church. PCA women have a definite freedom of ministry within the church's understanding of male and female roles. This is evidenced by the unity of spirit and purpose among all the parts.

NOTES:

1. John Calvin, *Calvin's Wisdom, An Anthology Arranged Alphabetically*, ed. Graham Miller (Carlisle, PA: The Banner of Truth Trust, 1992), 50-51.

2. Edmund P. Clowney, *Living in Christ's Church* (Philadelphia: Great Commission Publications, 1986), 7.

3. Jack Miller, *The Heart of a Servant Leader*, ed. Barbara Miller Juliani (Phillipsburg, NJ: P & R Publishing, 2004), 77.

The Need

Ephesians describes the church as God's new humanity, a colony in which the Lord of history has established a foretaste of the renewed unity and dignity of the human race . . . a community in which God's power to reconcile men and women to himself is experienced and then shared in transformed relationships. . . . It is an outpost in a dark world . . . offering light to the lost. . . . The church is a bride being prepared for the approach of her lover and husband.

SPIRIT OF THE REFORMATION STUDY BIBLE[1]

$\mathscr{T}$he role of women in God's Church is a vital and volatile question in every age, but the increased visibility of this topic in our time demands that the Church develop a theology of, and a functioning model for, women's ministry in the local church. Even among evangelicals who hold to male headship, there is widespread difference in practice regarding women's ministry.

• In some churches the women's ministry is event-, task-, or personality-driven. An inherent danger is that any ministry that is not biblically informed will eventually become competitive and divisive.

• Some churches do not have a women's ministry because of a concern or even experience that if women are organized, they will make demands and seek power. In this vacuum of isolation and underutilization of women there is the potential for frustration and anger-birthed leadership to erupt among the women, and the very thing the church is attempting to avoid becomes a reality.

• Some churches assert that women can do anything that unordained men can do. The proponents of this approach say that since women are mainstreamed into the total ministry of the church, a women's ministry is irrelevant or redundant. The vulnerability of this position is that it denies the uniqueness of woman's design and role and leaves men and women susceptible to egalitarianism. Without a biblical apologetic of womanhood, and a mechanism for women to be discipled by godly women, the church will imbibe the world's apologetic, and this distortion will create confusion and conflict among men and women.

A common weakness of these approaches is a failure to affirm and celebrate the *value* of God's creation design and redemptive calling of women and the *necessity* for woman's design and calling to be employed in the life and work of the church. Our concern is that many approaches to women's ministry are expedient and pragmatic responses to culture rather than thoughtful and intentional applications of Scripture.

COVENANTAL AND COMPLEMENTARIAN

The covenants of the Bible give the framework to understand Scripture. God's covenant of grace supplies the vital structure, the unifying thread, of His redemptive plan set forth in Scripture. The covenant of grace is the sovereignly initiated arrangement by which the Triune God lives in saving favor and merciful relationship with His people. Because we are in union with Him, we are united to His other children. So the covenant of grace defines our relationship to God and to one another. It orders a way of life that flows out of a promise of life. To realize this is to think and live covenantally.

Complementarianism gives the relational framework for men and women to live out their covenantal privileges and responsibilities. The complementarian position acknowledges that God created men and women equal in being but assigned different—but equally valuable—functions in His kingdom and that this gender distinctiveness complements, or harmonizes, to fulfill His purpose.

Complementarians believe that the Bible teaches that God has created men and women equal in their essential dignity and human personhood, but different and complementary in function—with male spiritual leadership in the home and believing community, the Church, being understood as a part of God's design. That means that both men and women are image-bearers of the living God. We are each fully human in all that entails. We are equals before the cross, brothers and sisters in our Lord Jesus Christ. But God has made us different. He has given certain functions and roles to men, and certain functions and roles to women, that are distinct.

By contrast, egalitarianism cannot come to grips with the uniquenesses of man created as male and female and asserts that there is no legitimate difference of role and function between men and women in the home and church, at least not one that allows for male spiritual leadership. Our conviction is that egalitarianism devalues God's creation design and redemptive calling of women. It fails to do justice to the distinctions that exist between men and women. It wrongly equates any acknowledgment of role distinctions with inequality and discrimination.

This book presents a covenantal and complementarian approach to womanhood and to women's ministry in the church. There is nothing more beautiful, satisfying, delightful, and God-glorifying than when men and women live and work together in complementarity.

SUSAN: WHY A CHURCH NEEDS AN APOLOGETIC ON BIBLICAL WOMANHOOD

Biblical womanhood and worldly womanhood are radically different, just as everything about the Christian life is countercultural and counterintuitive. Without a biblical apologetic for womanhood, individual women and women's ministries will lose their way. The following is a summary of the apologetic that is developed in the *Biblical Foundations for Womanhood* materials (see page 27). This apologetic is based on woman's creation design as a helper and her redemptive calling to be a life-giver.

The Triune God is a covenant-making, covenant-keeping God. So when He created man and woman in His own image, the covenantal imprint was stamped upon them. The personal and relational character of God demanded that His image-bearers be personal, relational beings. Thus He said, "It is not good that the man should be alone; I will make him a helper fit for him" (Genesis 2:18). When God presented her to the man, "the man said . . . 'she shall be called Woman'" (v. 23). "Adam's naming . . . expressed his authority, but paradoxically he named her 'woman,' implying that she was his equal."[2] The man and woman were created equally in God's image but designed for different functions.

The helper design is fascinating. The Hebrew word translated helper, *ezer*, is frequently used to refer to God as our Helper. These passages give insight into the function of an *ezer*.

• Exodus 18:4: "[Moses named his son] Eliezer (for he said, 'The God of my father was my help, and delivered me from the sword of Pharaoh')."

• Psalm 10:14: "But you do see, for you note mischief and vexation, that you may take it into your hands; to you the helpless commits himself; you have been the helper of the fatherless."

• Psalm 20:2: "May he send you help from the sanctuary and give you support from Zion."

• Psalm 33:20: "Our soul waits for the LORD; he is our help and our shield."

• Psalm 70:5: "But I am poor and needy; hasten to me, O God! You are my help and my deliverer; O LORD, do not delay!"

• Psalm 72:12-14: "For he delivers the needy when he calls, the poor and him who has no helper. He has pity on the weak and the needy, and saves the lives of the needy. From oppression and violence he redeems their life, and precious is their blood in his sight."

• Psalm 86:17: ". . . you, LORD, have helped me and comforted me."

When the man and woman sinned, Woman lost her ability to be a true helper. At this point of hopelessness, God gave hope. He promised that the woman's offspring would crush Satan's head (Genesis 3:15). Adam affirmed and celebrated his belief in this promise by renaming her. "The man called his wife's name Eve, because she was the mother of all living" (Genesis 3:20). Eve means "life-giver." Because of her rebellion the woman became a life-taker, but because of the promise of life she became a "life-giver." This is more than biological. Woman's redemptive calling is to be a life-giver in every relationship and circumstance.*

The following descriptions clarify woman's helper, life-giving ministry. The *ezer* words are strong, compassionate, relational, life-giving words.

HELPER/LIFE-GIVER	HINDERER/LIFE-TAKER
Exodus 18:4: Defends	attacks
Psalm 10:14: Sees, cares for oppressed	indifferent, unconcerned for oppressed
Psalm 20:2: Supports	weakens
Psalm 33:20: Shields, protects	leaves unprotected and defenseless
Psalm 70:5: Delivers from distress	causes distress
Psalm 72:12-14: Rescues poor, weak, needy	ignores poor, weak, needy
Psalm 86:17: Comforts	avoids, causes discomfort

Biblical womanhood is a covenantal concept. The helper design would be illogical in an autonomous vacuum. This design is nonsensical in a culture of self but is needful in a culture of covenant. The fifth-century Patriarch of Constantinople, John Chrysostom, wrote, "If they [the husband and wife] perform their proper duties, everything around them acquires firmness and stability."[3] When women join together to "perform their proper duties" as corporate helpers and life-givers in the family of God, they contribute to the firmness and stability of the Church.

When a church has a biblical apologetic for womanhood, the foundational concepts of woman's helper design and life-giving mission can permeate the women's ministry. Whether that ministry is small and informal or large and well-organized, it can be perpetually and intentionally guided by three questions:

- Are we being helpers or hinderers?
- Are we being life-givers or life-takers?
- Are we equipping women to be helpers and life-givers?

FOUNDATIONAL PRINCIPLES OF BIBLICAL WOMANHOOD*

The following summary of the principles developed in the *Biblical Foundations for Womanhood* materials is not an exhaustive list of what the

Bible teaches about womanhood, but it is sufficient to begin equipping women to understand this pertinent topic.

How are we related to God?

- God created us in His image (Genesis 1:26-27).
- God is our reference point (Deuteronomy 6:4-5).
- God's Word is our authority (Deuteronomy 6:6-9).
- God's glory is our purpose (Isaiah 43:7).

How does Scripture define womanhood?

- Woman's helper design and life-giving mission are creational and covenantal concepts (Genesis 2:18; 3:20).
- Woman's helper ministry can be summarized as community and compassion (Psalm 144:12).
- Because of the Fall, woman cannot fulfill her creation design or accomplish her covenantal mission (Genesis 3:8).
- Through redemption in Christ, woman's ability to be and do what she was created to be and do is restored (Genesis 3:15-16).
- A redeemed woman is to be equipped to fulfill her design and mission through the ministry of the church (Titus 2:1, 3-5).
- Woman must lose her life in order to be a life-giver (Luke 17:33).
- Woman's confident hope in God produces the enduring beauty of a quiet and gentle spirit (1 Peter 3:1-6).

How are we related to others?

- The church is the covenant community (Exodus 19:4-6; 1 Peter 2:9-10).
- God created men and women equal in being but with diversity of function (1 Timothy 2:9-15).
- God's kingdom order of male headship is good (Genesis 1:31; Psalm 119:68).
- Submission in marriage and in the Church is an acceptance of God's kingdom order (1 Peter 3:1-6).
- Women are to pass the legacy of biblical womanhood on to the next generation (Titus 2:1, 3-5).

LIGON: WHY A CHURCH NEEDS A WOMEN'S MINISTRY

In our feminist, egalitarian culture, wise pastors and godly Christian women involved in ministry to women realize that the preaching, teaching, and discipleship ministry of the local church needs to do at least five things in connection with promoting a practical embrace of biblical womanhood in the congregation.

(1) We need to cultivate godly, feminine, Christian women. But this can't happen if the church in its teaching underemphasizes the differences between men and women or denies the differences in male-female role relationships.

(2) We need to promote healthy Christian marriages. But this can't happen if the church in its teaching doesn't deal biblically with the respective roles of husband and wife. The ways that husbands and wives relate to one another are not identical, though they are complementary. Hence, learning the biblical distinctions in our mutual marital responsibilities and the different ways we are to relate to one another as husbands and wives is vital and essential to furthering biblical, holy, and happy marriages. This means that egalitarianism, whether explicit or implicit, witting or unwitting, is part of the disintegration of marriage in our culture.

(3) We need, more specifically, to promote godly, monogamous, heterosexual marriages. But this can't happen if the church doesn't have a consistent method of biblical interpretation in support of its teaching ministry. For instance, if there are no gender-related distinctions between male and female roles in marriage, then why should marriage be conceived as only between a man and woman? Why not homosexual marriage? The evangelical feminist has no good answer for this. Complementarians do!

(4) We need to cultivate among our Christian women a joyous embrace of godly, healthy, Christian, male spiritual leadership in the church. But this will never happen unless ministers and other church leaders believe *and teach the local church* what the Bible says about qualified male church leadership. The claims of Christian egalitarians are becoming more pronounced and histrionic in this area. Qualified male church leadership is being called "domination" and "abuse." Meanwhile,

many evangelicals, stung by the criticism of chauvinism, wanting to placate the culture's suspicion of the church's teaching on an all-male clergy, desiring to reach a hostile culture without "turning it off" with unpopular views, not to mention wanting to avoid controversy in their own congregation with the unconvinced, are downplaying this biblical teaching. They believe it but don't preach and teach it, and they do their best to disguise it in local church life. However, a vital aspect to healthy New Testament church life is lost when this principle is ignored.

(5) We need to help Christian women appreciate the manifold areas of service that are open to them in the church and to equip them distinctively as women to fulfill their ministry. But this will never happen if our approach to discipleship in the church is androgynous—that is, if it refuses to take into account the gender distinctives of the disciple. And it will never happen if we are not brave enough to address the Bible's teaching on male-female roles and functions in the home and church.

In light of these important needs and goals, we offer some key reasons why a distinctive discipleship of women is important in the congregation.

Five Reasons Why Women's Ministry Is Important in Every Healthy Evangelical Church

First, women's ministry is important because through it we have the opportunity to address helpfully the issue of the nature of manhood and womanhood, an issue that is very much at the heart of the cultural transition that we find ourselves in the midst of right now. Male/female role relationships, the definition of the family, homosexual rights—all of these are bellwether issues of our culture. Behind the shifts in our society's attitude to these issues is a worldview megashift moving from a Judeo-Christian or biblical framework to a pagan worldview. Until about 1970 we had been operating from the residue of a Christian worldview; since that time we have seen a dramatic and rapid shift to an essentially pagan worldview. Unfortunately, one way this pagan framework is being actively imported into the church by self-avowed Christian leaders is through their compromise on the subject of biblical manhood and womanhood. Bruce Ware, professor of theology at Southern Baptist Seminary, says:

Today . . . the primary areas in which Christianity is pressured to conform are on issues of *gender* and *sexuality*. Postmoderns and ethical relativists care little about doctrinal truth claims; these seem to them innocuous, archaic, and irrelevant to life. What they *do* care about, and care with a vengeance, is whether their feminist agenda and sexual perversions are tolerated, endorsed and expanded in an increasingly neopagan landscape. Because this is what they care most about, it is precisely here that Christianity is most vulnerable. To lose the battle here is to subject the Church to increasing layers of departure from biblical faith. And surely, it will not be long until ethical departures (the Church yielding to feminist pressures for women's ordination, for example) will yield even more central doctrinal departures (questioning whether Scripture's inherent patriarchy renders it fundamentally untrustworthy, for example). I find it instructive that when Paul warns about departures from the faith in the latter days, he lists ethical compromises and the searing of the conscience as the prelude to a full-scale doctrinal apostasy (1 Tim 4:1-5).[4]

Ethical compromise comes first, then the doctrinal sellout follows. We evangelicals care about doctrine. The cultural progressives don't. But if we capitulate to their ethical reordering, doctrinal unfaithfulness is certain to follow.

Second, it is important that we have a deliberate, intentional ministry to women in the church because the Bible teaches so much and so clearly on manhood and womanhood. It is never, ever safe to act unbiblically or to ignore biblical teaching, and the Bible says so much about the way that men and women are to relate, especially in the home and in the church. A church that wants to be biblical, then, will want to make sure the women of the congregation embrace and implement this teaching. And there is no better way for us to discreetly and appropriately address those nitty-gritty issues than in the context of a women's ministry. Without in any way discounting the regular pulpit ministry of the church, we should recognize that there are certain matters more aptly addressed and applied in the context of a specific discipleship of women, whether in large groups, in small groups, or in situations of confidentiality, as women minister to women.

Third, women's ministry is important because when biblical manhood and womanhood are denied or altered or unpracticed, that results in disasters for marriages, families, and churches. Unbiblical husband/wife relations can lead not only to marital failures but to gender confusion in children and first-order societal problems. We see this everywhere today. Women's ministry provides a safe and secure environment where those kinds of things can be addressed. For instance, many marriages suffer continuous tension because the husband and wife lack an understanding of (or perhaps have a positive disagreement about) the biblical teaching on role relationships in the home. Women's ministry gives us a unique opportunity to grapple with these things in the kind of practical detail that will help the health and welfare of Christian marriages, and thus local churches.

Fourth, we ought to have an intentional, deliberate approach to female discipleship because men and women are different, and these differences need to be recognized, taken into account, and addressed in the course of Christian discipleship. This, as we have already noted, is something with which egalitarians cannot come helpfully to grips. The difference, the distinctness of men and women, is not only obviously displayed to us physiologically, biologically, and psychologically, it is written plainly for us on the opening pages of the Bible. When God created man, Moses tells us, He created them "male and female" (Genesis 1:27). This universal, creational reality has implications for discipleship.

It means that the distinction between male and female is something that is part of a human's (and especially a Christian's) being a bearer of the image of God. Think about it. Our God is one and yet eternally exists in three persons—Father, Son, and Holy Spirit. Our triune God is both equal and distinct, the archetype of the true individual and true community. Mankind, without living out the God-given distinction of male and female, relating to one another as God intended them to relate, cannot give adequate expression to this aspect of what it means to be created in the image of God. This truth needs to be explained and understood in the discipleship of the local church.

The universal, creational reality also means that our response to faithful biblical proclamation about God's design for male and female role relationships, and to the recognition of differences between men and women and how they work out in God's order for the home and church, should be *"Vive le difference!"* It's wonderful! This is not something to apologize for, nor something to be ashamed of in our postmodern culture, but rather this is the way God made us to be and live, and it's better than any other way. It is good. But it is so radically countercultural that it needs to be inculcated, specifically and explicitly, to men and women in the local church.

One way that these differences work out in the lives of Christian men and women is in the area of temptation. Men and women face different kinds of temptations differently. Thus the local church needs to address these distinctive temptations of men and women distinctively. And this is one purpose of intentional, deliberate ministry to women in the local congregation.

Of course, all of these points speak to the relevance of a distinctive discipleship of Christian men in the church, but they also indicate why we need to be self-conscious in our ministry to Christian women.

Fifth, the denial or the twisting of the Bible's clear teaching on manhood and womanhood is one of the central ways that biblical authority is being undermined in our times. That's why Bruce Ware has said, "To the extent that [giving in on these issues of gender and sexuality] occurs, the church establishes a pattern of following cultural pressures and urgings against the clear authority of God's written word. When this happens . . . the church becomes desensitized to Scripture's radical call and forms, instead, a taste for worldly accolades. . . . To compromise on a little thing will pave the way for compromises on much that matters."[5]

The church has been called to shape culture, not ape it. But very often our churches reflect rather than constructively influence worldly culture. Even worse, some church leaders tell us that if we want to reach the culture, we must become like the culture. Don't you love the way Dorothy Sayers confronted this mixed-up notion? She said: "It is not the business of the church to conform Christ to men, but men to Christ."[6] That's precisely the challenge we face in the area of biblical manhood and womanhood. Will the church conform her values to the prevailing cultural mores and norms, or will we impact and influence and shape our culture?

Of course, behind and underneath this is the fundamental issue of biblical authority. If you can write off, ignore, or distort the Bible's teaching in this area, as crystal-clear as it is, then you can do so with anything the Bible teaches. Indeed, the Bible is so clear and blunt on this that sometimes it is hard for ministers to stand in the pulpit and read aloud certain biblical passages, knowing the kind of reaction they may provoke in hearers who have been steeped in a feminist culture alien to the biblical-complementarian thought-world of the Scriptures. But if you can change what the Bible says on this, you can make the Bible say whatever you want it to say. Thus the manhood-womanhood issue becomes a scriptural authority issue. Is our pattern in the church going to be a hermeneutical twist whenever the Bible's teaching makes us culturally uncomfortable about an issue, or are we going to let the lion loose, let God be God, and let his Word speak and rule in our lives? So, fundamentally this is a scriptural authority issue. In Part 2, Susan will discuss how a women's ministry has the capacity to deal with this issue in a unique way.

THE DANGEROUS SILENCE OF THE CHURCH

The crisis of womanhood is too critical for the church to be passive. Scores of evangelical women are functional feminists, because the world's paradigm for womanhood is the only one they have heard. The church should lead the way in equipping God's people to think biblically about all of life, including a biblical perspective of gender roles and relationships.

It is not sufficient for churches that hold to male headship simply to compile a list of things that are *permissible* for women to do. We must go to the Scriptures and determine what is *needful* for women to do. God pronounced gender-aloneness "not good" in the Garden, and the same is true in the church. He did not give His benediction of "It is very good" until man and woman stood side by side, equal but different.

The church must boldly articulate a robustly positive perspective of womanhood and of woman's role in the church, and the church must equip godly older women to disciple younger women to think and live according to this perspective. If a local church remains silent on this issue, women are unequipped to fulfill their covenantal calling.

This pastor remains anonymous, but he represents many who have had similar experiences.

For decades our church was silent about the design and calling of women, and we are reaping the results. The women's ministry operated with a high degree of skill, but also a high degree of independence. It was separate from the other ministries in the church and not accountable to the elders. The women have used Bible studies that are not consistent with the doctrines of the church. Strong personalities have led the ministry, and there have been significant numbers of women who chose not to be involved rather than risk conflict with these leaders. As a result our older women are not equipped to disciple, and younger women are unaware of their need to be discipled by older women. Many aspects of church life suffered. When the elders realized the consequences of our neglect and tried to slowly and gently bring the women's ministry back into the mainstream of the church, we were met with resistance and criticism. This saddened us because it is an indication that the women do not have a healthy doctrine of the church, nor do they understand biblical principles of womanhood. The upheaval has been painful, but we are committed to rescuing this ministry because we value and need the ministry of women. By God's grace, we are prayerfully assuming our responsibility to the women of our church. We are grateful that God's Word shows us the way.

---

* *Biblical Foundations for Womanhood* resources that amplify concepts in this chapter:

Woman's creation design as a helper and her redemptive calling to be a life-giver: *The Legacy of Biblical Womanhood*, Chapters 1—10.

"Foundational Principles of Biblical Womanhood": This list is developed in the Leader's Guide for *The Legacy of Biblical Womanhood*.

NOTES:

1. *Spirit of the Reformation Study Bible* (Grand Rapids, MI: Zondervan, 2003), 1903.
2. Ibid., 12.
3. Quoted in Edward A. Hartman, *Homeward Bound* (Ross-shire, UK: Christian Focus Publications, 2001), 30. Quoted from *Puritan Sermons, 1659-1689*, Vol. 2 (1674; reprint: Wheaton, IL: Richard Owen Roberts, 1981), 303.
4. Bruce A. Ware, "Ethics in a New Millennium," *The Southern Baptist Journal of Theology* 4, No. 1 (Spring 2000): 91-92.
5. Ibid., 92.
6. Dorothy Sayers, *Creed or Chaos* (1940; reprint: Manchester, NH: Sophia Institute Press, 1996), 24-25.

3

The Motive

Every Christian should have his Church enclosed within his heart, and be affected with its maladies, as if they were his own,—sympathize with its sorrows, and bewail its sins.

JOHN CALVIN[1]

A NOTE FROM SUSAN

This chapter is adapted from a sermon Ligon preached at a women's leadership conference, and I particularly wanted him to include it in this book. The principles are the same for men and women, but it was preached specifically to women. It was electrifying for us as we were challenged to fall in love with the church. My prayer is that your heart will beat as wildly as mine did as you reflect on the unspeakable privilege of being the bride of Christ, and that this sermon will prepare you for the countercultural call to women in God's church that will unfold in Part 2 of this book.

THE SERMON — FALLING IN LOVE WITH THE CHURCH

The only reliable motive for encouraging women's ministry in the local church is an insatiable longing to see the display of God's glory in the local church. But God's vision of the church has fallen on hard soil in our time. Christians show little appreciation for the importance of the local church and little zeal for its essential role in Christian discipleship and in bearing witness to a lost world of the reality of gospel community.

We need to reorient ourselves by the Word of God and embrace His attitude toward and vision for the local church. This radical reorientation must be based upon what the Church is and who the Savior of the Church is.

Without a proper esteem and love for Christ Himself, and an understanding of His covenant love for His church, we will lack the motive-force to serve Him in the world. If our ultimate motivation for service to God is simply because we love people, we will never be able to sustain the call to service that God has given to us because the very people we are called to serve will break our hearts. It is only the grace of Christ that enables us to persevere.

ECCLESIOLOGY 101

Ecclesiology simply means what the Bible teaches about the church. Without a strong ecclesiology we will not see the church as God sees her. The ugliness of the life of the church in a fallen world will blind us to the glorious beauty that is the assembly of the living God, the fellowship of the saints, the Body of Christ, the Church of our God and Savior.

If we're not captivated by the beauty and significance of the church, we will lack the motive-force to serve her because when we begin to serve God's people we quickly discover that they hurt and disappoint us. A biblical ecclesiology reminds us that we have the privilege of following in our Savior's footsteps and loving those who are not in and of themselves lovely. Scripture reminds us that it is God's design to make them altogether lovely, and He invites us to serve Him by contributing to the preparation of His bride to meet Him at the marriage supper of the Lamb. There she will be perfect, without spot and blameless, with great beauty and glory.

Throughout the remainder of this book we will use the Pastoral Letters, 1 and 2 Timothy and Titus, to examine God's call to women to serve Him in His church and His call to the church to prepare women for this mission. But before we consider this twofold call, we need a biblical ecclesiology. Paul provides this in his first letter to Timothy.

First Timothy 3:14-16

> *I hope to come to you soon, but I am writing these things to you so that, if I delay, you may know how one ought to behave in the household of God, which is the church of the living God, a pillar and buttress of truth. Great indeed, we confess, is the mystery of godliness: He was manifested in the flesh, vindicated by the Spirit, seen by angels, proclaimed among the nations, believed on in the world, taken up in glory.*

In verses 1-5 Paul discussed the character and qualifications of elders and deacons. You can imagine how overwhelming it would be to these men to hear the qualifications that God requires of them. So in verses 14-16 Paul tells them to take their eyes off of those demands and to look at the church and her Savior. Our own sense of insufficiency and our hesitancy to obey the demands of church life will be dealt with as we turn our eyes to the glory of the bride of Christ and to the glory of Christ Himself. So Paul asserts great truths about what the church is and about the nature, character, and person of Christ.

We will consider three truths from this passage that give the foundation for a strong doctrine of the church and that have radical implications for the ministry of women in the church: the Bible, the church, and Christ.

The Bible: "I am writing these things to you so that, if I delay, you may know how one ought to behave in the household of God, which is the church of the living God"(v. 15).

The reason Paul wrote this letter is so that we will know how to behave in the local church. Paul's great concern in all the Pastoral Letters is for us to do church the way God wants us to do church. He wants us to grow in grace the way God wants us to grow in grace. That's why he draws our attention, first, to the Scripture when he says, "I am writing these things . . ."

The words Paul wrote are part of the Holy Scriptures. In his second letter to Timothy he explained that all Scripture is given by inspiration and is profitable for reproof, correction, and training in righteousness, that we might be equipped for every good work (3:16-17). The Bible is to have a controlling influence in our lives and in our ministry in the local church. At the heart of Paul's practical instructions in this letter—

practical instructions about the goal of teaching, the law in the Christian life, prayer, male and female role relationships in the church, and the qualifications of church officers—is a call to the local congregation to live in light of the enormous truth that we are God's church. We are His house, His family, His gathered people. The people and the house we serve are not ours; they are His. It is vital that we live and minister in accordance with His Book. This is completely counterintuitive in our pragmatic culture. We want to minister *our* way. We want to set up our own rules and define the game plan. But Paul emphasizes that if we are to grow in grace as a congregation, if we are to be what He has called us to be, we have to live and minister according to the Book.

Sisters in Christ, I challenge you to regularly encourage your ministers and elders to be faithful to Scripture, especially in the areas that they are most afraid to touch. Frankly, one of those areas is male/female role relationships in the home and in the church. Some good and godly ministers and elders are somewhat intimidated about declaring the truth of God in these areas precisely because they respect their sisters in Christ. They fear that they will appear to look down on women or to think of themselves as superior or to have fallen into some sort of traditional chauvinism. Women have the opportunity to encourage them by repeatedly saying, "We expect you to teach us the full teachings of God's Word, even when it is uncomfortable for us and even when it is not politically correct. We want to hear all that God has to say to us."

The church: ". . . the household of God, which is the church of the living God, a pillar and buttress of truth" (1 Timothy 3:15).

Paul wants us to be crystal-clear about the nature of the church. In this verse he is especially thinking of the local congregation of gathered believers. He wants us to have a proper estimation of and love for the church, so he zeroes in on three qualities of the church.

First, he calls the church "the household of God." The local church is the family of God. This letter was first read to the members of the church in Ephesus, which was founded by the apostle Paul and pastored by Timothy. We don't know how many were there, but when Paul used this familial language he was saying to Timothy, "I want you to realize when you look out on those people God has gathered that you are looking at the family He has chosen for Himself. Live and minister realizing that those people are God's kin."

I grew up in the South, and Southerners take their children to graveyards to meet their kin. I remember standing among the gravestones and my father saying, "Son, these are your people." The long genealogical discourse and historical lecture that followed gave me a sense that generation after generation after generation had told the next generation about the glories of the Lord, and I was the undeserving recipient and beneficiary of that great covenantal legacy. Paul was saying to Timothy, "When you look out among that little group of people huddled in that house church, remember that they are God's people. Take care of them, and never underestimate how glorious they are."

Second, Paul adds that this household is "the church of the living God." This is Old Testament language. The word translated *church* is a Greek rendering of the Hebrew word *qahal*, which was used for the assembly of the Lord. One of the first places this assembling took place was at Sinai (Exodus 20). God Himself spoke to the people, and the thunder and lightning and trumpets were so powerful that the people stampeded from the mountain in terror. They begged Moses, "You speak to us, and we will listen; but do not let God speak to us, lest we die." They had come into the presence of the living God, and it was awesome. Paul reminded Timothy that the handful of people gathered in Ephesus were the assembly of the living God. Jesus Christ said, "Where two or three are gathered in my name, there am I among them" (Matthew 18:20). When the church gathers in Jesus' name by His Spirit and according to His Word, to bring Him worship, He is as present with them as He was at Sinai. They are the assembly of the living God.

Third, Paul refers to the church as "a pillar and buttress of truth." The Church is the essential vehicle of evangelism and discipleship and the defender of the faith. The privilege of preserving and propagating the gospel was entrusted to the church by Jesus when He said, "All authority in heaven and on earth has been given to me. Go therefore and make disciples of all nations, baptizing them . . ." (Matthew 28:18-19). One of the things this means is that discipleship is to take place in the local church because that is where you baptize. The local congregation is where the truth is communicated to the next generation. The local church is where God especially meets with His people in the new-covenant era, and it is the essential instrument through which He propagates the truth.

The last thing that the pillar and buttress of truth should ever do is capitulate to culture. Yet some of the most creative energies being poured into the expansion of the Church in North America today are committed to the principle that the way you reach the culture is to become like it. This passage fortifies us to understand God's design for the local church. A strong ecclesiology is essential because in our ministry we never see the church as she fully ought to be. A dear Scottish professor of mine was preaching in the west Highlands of Scotland, and afterward a godly old woman said to him, "Professor Macleod, I just want to say that the older I grow, the more I love the Lord's people. . . ." And as he was thinking, *Oh, isn't that sweet*, she added, ". . . and the less I trust them." Her ecclesiology taught her that the Lord's people will hurt you, but they are His people. She understood that when her heart was broken from pouring herself into ministry, she had the privilege of being like the Lord Jesus Christ who laid down His life for a recalcitrant church that hurt Him.

Christ: "Great indeed, we confess, is the mystery of godliness: He was manifested in the flesh, vindicated by the Spirit, seen by angels, proclaimed among the nations, believed on in the world, taken up in glory" (v. 16).

Ultimately, the basis of our ecclesiology is Christ. Paul's concern is godliness among these Christians. He wants them to be biblical, not worldly. He wants them to be gracious, truth-loving, Christ-loving, distinct disciples who are growing in the grace and knowledge of Jesus. Where do you point someone for that? You show them Jesus.

He begins by referring to the mystery of godliness, and we expect four easy steps to complete sanctification in seven days or less. But the great mystery is . . . "*He*." The secret of the Christian life is Christ. He is the mystery of godliness. He is the One whose ministry will make His people godly and who will make His church godly. Godliness here refers to the active godliness of the Christian life whereby we minister and serve one another. The great mystery of our new life and obedience is Jesus Christ.

John Owen, the great Puritan theologian, teacher, and vice chancellor of the University of Oxford, wrote twenty-four volumes of theology in tiny print and elephantine English. After reflecting upon God's teaching about the church for the whole of his life, he said that all pastoral ministry basically boils down to two things: making those who are not in union with Christ to know that they are not in union with Christ, and making those who are in union with Christ to live as if they are in union with Christ.

In this text the apostle Paul tells Christians—those who rest and trust on Jesus Christ alone for salvation—to live in their union with Christ.

The citizens of Ephesus had a little chant: "Great is Artemis of the Ephesians!" (Acts 19:28, 34). Artemis was the pet god of the Ephesians. Paul is intentionally countercultural when he gives the Ephesian Christians their motto: "Great is the mystery of godliness—Christ."

Paul answers the question of the life of grace and of ministry in the local church theologically and Christologically. He asserts that Christ is the source, the revelation, the example of our godliness; so our godliness and our obedience are rooted in Him. His purpose is to give us a vision of the Master. His design is to stoke our love for Christ because the Christian must serve in utter dependence on and with a deep love for Jesus Christ. We must be caught up in His grace and His glory. In six grand phrases he pictures our glorious Lord.

"He was manifested in the flesh." This points to the incarnation of Christ. Though He had existed in glory with the Father, He came to earth and was humiliated in His life and ministry and death.

He was *"vindicated by the Spirit."* The Holy Spirit testified that Jesus' life, ministry, and resurrection comprised the very picture of God. Indeed He was God Himself in the flesh.

He was *"seen by angels."* Paul points to Christ's angelic witness. Perhaps he is reminding us of the angels who witnessed Jesus' resurrection.

He was *"proclaimed among the nations."* Imagine how encouraging this would have been to the little group of Christians who were a persecuted minority compared to the wealthy and powerful in the city of

Ephesus. They would have been emboldened to know that the name of Jesus was being carried into all the nations.

He was "believed on in the world." Not only was He proclaimed throughout the world, but there was worldwide worship of Jesus Christ. He is the Savior of the world, and all kinds and classes and types of men and women trust in Him.

He was "taken up in glory." Jesus' ascension witnesses to His claims and reminds us that He is God. He ascended to the right hand of God the Father Almighty, and He ever lives to intercede for and rule His church by His word and Spirit and to uphold all things by the word of His power.

Paul intends for us to draw encouragement from these magnificent truths about Jesus Christ. William Guthrie once said of Jesus, "Less would not satisfy, more is not desired."[2]

Scripture calls us to things that are utterly counterintuitive, utterly countercultural, and demanding in the extreme, but Scripture shows us the Savior and His bride. This glorious sight motivates us to live under God's authority and to serve Him through the local church, for His glory and our good. Falling in love with Christ means falling in love with His Church.

A biblical women's ministry will teach women to love the church. But how are women to respond when the local church does not love women or women's ministry? We asked several women who have experienced this to share their thoughts. The following compilation represents various situations, but the triumphant theme is the grace of God enabling these women to remain constant in their love for Christ and His Church.

It is painful when elders do not consider the women's ministry worthy of their time and leadership. It is confusing when they do not support or promote women's ministry. At times I wonder if they really believe that the differences between men and women should be celebrated and encouraged or if they agree with the world's opinion that there are no differences in roles between men and women. How are women to love the church when they feel unloved by the church? I have found the answer in Scripture's admonition to women who are married to unbelieving or disobedient husbands. The failure or weakness of male leadership does not absolve us of our responsibility. We are to run to the Author and Perfecter of our faith with our hurts, wounds, and disappointments. We are to see this season as a part of our individual and corporate sanctification offered by our sovereign God who loves us steadfastly.

When women are scorned and disrespected by philosophies of ministry that denigrate the design, calling, and roles of women, we are tempted to react with militant defensiveness. Scripture calls us to remember that Jesus, the King of the Church, delights in us. We are not called to defend ourselves but to defend Christ's Kingdom through prayer and service.

Women need a time and place where they can learn about biblical womanhood and lovingly challenge each other when behaviors reflect worldly attitudes. When young women learn more about womanhood from TV, movies, magazines, and the Internet than they do from mature older women, they will often make unbiblical decisions. I did, but then I experienced the difference it makes to have spiritual mothers to guide me. I continue to serve in women's ministry, even though it is marginalized in my church, because I am a different woman today because of the love and wisdom that women poured into my life.

As the leader of the women's ministry in our church, I have felt disappointed, rejected, abandoned, and disrespected, and I have often responded in all the wrong ways. I have been angry and defensive. I have been tempted to withdraw, or to engage in militant recruitment of women who will see it my way. I am grateful that our great and gracious God does not abandon or reject me. He pursues me with grace, mercy, and peace. He continues what He has accomplished by excising this hurt, angry, rebellious heart and giving me a new heart to know Him, obey Him, and love what and whom He loves. My prayer is not that I will love the Church in some global sense but that He will give me particular love for the place and people where He has assigned me.

NOTES:

1. John Calvin, *Calvin's Wisdom, An Anthology Arranged Alphabetically*, ed. Graham Miller (Carlisle, PA: The Banner of Truth Trust, 1992), 56.
2. William Guthrie, *The Christian's Great Interest* (Edinburgh: The Banner of Truth Trust, 1994), 52.

Part 2

THE APOLOGETIC

$\mathscr{N}$OTE FROM LIGON

In this section Susan will examine passages in the Pastoral Epistles that deal specifically with women's role in the church. These passages provide principles that will help answer the questions posed by this book.

- Why should a church have a women's ministry—what is the biblical apologetic?

- Who is responsible for the women's ministry in a church?

- How does a women's ministry relate to the other ministries in the church?

- What are the tasks of a women's ministry?

- How does a church implement a biblical approach to women's ministry?

4

Foundations

The relationship of Christ to the church is so varied and rich as to defy adequate description. . . . He is both its founder and its foundation, its savior and its owner, its preserver and its hope, its lover and its beloved, its righteousness and its holiness, its Head and its King. . . . He is transcendently glorious. And His body, the church, cannot but partake of His glory.

R. B. KUIPER[1]

THE TEXTS: 1 AND 2 TIMOTHY, TITUS

There is no chapter and verse that mandates a women's ministry in the church. Neither is there a specific directive for a Sunday school, mercy committee, missions committee, or church treasurer. However, there are commands to disciple God's people, minister to the oppressed, take the gospel to the world, and be good stewards of financial resources. And there are principles upon which a church can develop structures to obey these commands.

The letters to Timothy and Titus are known as the Pastoral Letters because they were written to these men in their capacity as pastors of churches. The apostle Paul planted a church in Ephesus and then sent Timothy there to serve as pastor. He left Titus on the island of Crete to serve the church Paul had begun there. Paul had developed the doctrine of the Church in the letter to the Ephesians, but these pastoral letters deal with the practical theology of pastoral care and oversight of the Church.

They give solid principles for the organization and covenant life of the Church, including the role and responsibilities of women.

Paul stated his purpose clearly:

> *I hope to come to you soon, but I am writing these things to you so that, if I delay, you may know how one ought to behave in the household of God, which is the church of the living God, the pillar and buttress of truth.* (1 Timothy 3:14-15)

Before we consider the specific texts that relate to women in the church, we will look at some of the overarching, foundational truths that form the fabric of these letters. Unless each text is seen in this context, the principles concerning women will be diminished and distorted.

Foundational Theme #1: The Gospel

These letters are laced with magnificent doxologies to the grace of God in Christ. These theological meditations equip us to think biblically. Titus 3:4-7 is a sterling example:

> *But when the goodness and loving kindness of God our Savior appeared, he saved us, not because of works done by us in righteousness, but according to his own mercy, by the washing of regeneration and renewal of the Holy Spirit, whom he poured out on us richly through Jesus Christ our Savior, so that being justified by his grace we might become heirs according to the hope of eternal life.*

John Stott says that this passage "is perhaps the fullest statement of salvation in the New Testament."[2]

Paul viewed everything from a biblical perspective, including his instructions regarding women. Whether we see these instructions as splendid or severe will depend on our mind-set. Christ, not womanhood or the women's ministry, must be the reference point. Unless a women's ministry is an overflow of the gospel, women will become hinderers and not helpers in God's Church. Those who plan for and implement a women's ministry must be intentional in maintaining a gospel orientation in their hearts and lives.

Foundational Theme #2: Truth

As in every age, the early church faced the problem of false teachers who taught a false gospel. Paul's passion for truth is palpable. John Stott writes:

> The apostle's overriding preoccupation throughout all three Pastoral Letters is with the truth, that it may be faithfully guarded and handed on. The pertinence of this theme, at the end of the twentieth century, is evident. For contemporary culture is being overtaken and submerged by the spirit of postmodernism. Postmodernism begins as a self-conscious reaction against the modernism of the Enlightenment, and especially against its unbounded confidence in reason, science and progress. The postmodern mind rightly rejects this naive optimism. But it then goes further and declares that there is no such thing as objective or universal truth; that all so-called "truth" is purely subjective, being culturally conditioned; and that therefore we all have our own truth, which has as much right to respect as anybody else's.[3]

The truth about womanhood has been culturally conditioned. At a conference a young college woman asked, "How can I think biblically about womanhood when I am constantly told to pursue my own dreams, to be true to myself, and to seek my own fulfillment?" I encouraged her to become involved in the women's ministry in her church, to develop relationships with godly women, and to give them permission to speak the truth about womanhood into her life. But this solution presupposes that the church is equipping women for this ministry and that there is a delivery system—a women's ministry—to connect young women to wise older women.

Foundational Theme #3: Sound Doctrine

Because of the lurking danger of false doctrine, Paul put heavy emphasis on sound doctrine. Sound doctrine is the antidote for error. *Sound*, which is a key word in these letters, is translated from a Greek word that means whole or healthy. "Christian doctrine is healthy in the same way as the human body is healthy. For Christian doctrine resembles the human body. It is a coordinated system consisting of different parts which relate to one another and together constitute a harmonious whole. If therefore our theology is maimed (with bits missing) or diseased (with bits distorted), it is not 'sound' or 'healthy.'"[4]

Paul taught the young preachers the necessity of sound doctrine and ecclesiology. He wrote that an elder "must hold firm to the trustworthy word as taught, so that he may be able to give instruction in sound doctrine and also to rebuke those who contradict it" (Titus 1:9).

Paul stated unequivocally that it is in the context of healthy doctrine and ecclesiology that we can engage in healthy discipleship relationships. "But as for you [Titus], teach what accords with sound doctrine. . . . Older women . . . are to teach what is good, and so train the young women . . ."(Titus 2:1, 3-4)

A biblical approach to women's ministry demands a context of sound doctrine and sound ecclesiology. When a women's ministry exists within a "harmonious whole" of sound preaching and sound church government, women can be equipped to articulate a biblical apologetic of womanhood in word and deed.

Foundational Theme # 4: Discipleship

The emphasis on Christian education, or discipleship, is striking. A close reading of the letters not only reveals a cerebral strategy for the Christian education of a congregation but also shows the warm, relational aspect of biblical discipleship. The tender relationship between Paul and these two pastors is the model. He refers to them as his true sons, showing that spiritual mothering and fathering relationships should characterize the covenant community. This is the substance and the form of true biblical discipleship—a balanced blend of sound doctrine taught in the context of covenant relationships that reflect that doctrine. If we overemphasize content, the ministry will be academic. If the emphasis is only relational, the ministry will be anemic. Paul cogently described this healthy synthesis.*

> But we were gentle among you, like a nursing mother taking care of her own children. So, being affectionately desirous of you, we were ready to share with you not only the gospel of God but also our own selves, because you had become very dear to us. (1 Thessalonians 2:7-8)

Titus 2:3-5 instructs the pastor to equip older women to train younger women. If this mandate is disconnected from a biblical perspective of discipleship, it can easily become a purely relational model that magnifies the relationship rather than God's glory, or an academic model that elevates knowledge over the application of the gospel into life.*

Foundational Theme #5: Covenant

The covenant of grace is the unifying theme of these letters and, indeed, of all Scripture. All of the principles coalesce in this truth. It is poignantly obvious in 2 Timothy, which was written during Paul's final imprisonment as he awaited his execution.

> *Paul, an apostle of Christ Jesus by the will of God according to the promise of the life that is in Christ Jesus, To Timothy, my beloved child: Grace, mercy, and peace from God the Father and Christ Jesus our Lord. I thank God whom I serve, as did my ancestors, with a clear conscience, as I remember you constantly in my prayers night and day. As I remember your tears, I long to see you, that I may be filled with joy. I am reminded of your sincere faith, a faith that dwelt first in your grandmother Lois and your mother Eunice and now, I am sure, dwells in you as well. (1:1-5)*

This passage is packed with concepts that characterize the covenant of grace. Paul's reference to "the promise of . . . life" catapults us back to before the beginning when God "saved us and called us to a holy calling, not because of our works but because of his own purpose and grace, which he gave us in Christ Jesus before the ages began" (v. 9) and to the Garden when

> *The LORD God formed the man of dust from the ground and breathed into his nostrils the breath of life, and the man became a living creature. . . . And the LORD God commanded the man, saying, "You may surely eat of every tree of the garden, but of the tree of the knowledge of good and evil you shall not eat, for in the day that you eat of it you shall surely die." (Genesis 2:7, 16)*

The man and woman ate, and then they "hid themselves from the presence of the LORD God. . . . But the LORD God called to the man" (3:8-9). This is the story of redemption—man hiding and God seeking. God called to the man—and He calls us—because of His grace. *The covenant is sovereignly initiated.*

The man and woman listened as God spoke to the serpent: "I will put enmity between you and the woman . . ." (Genesis 3:15). They heard the Lord God say that He would do for them what they could not do for themselves. They could not disentangle themselves from the enemy of their souls, and neither can we. We are in need of grace because we can do nothing to merit life. "For the wages of sin is death, but the free gift of God is eternal life in Christ Jesus our Lord" (Romans 6:23). *The covenant is restorative.*

Surely Adam and Eve were awestruck as God continued, ". . . and between your offspring and her offspring; he shall bruise your head, and you shall bruise his heel" (Genesis 3:15). God would rescue them from their enemy and give them life. Sometime, somewhere the woman's offspring would defeat this enemy. When God promised to crush the head of the enemy, He bound Himself to His people in covenant loyalty. Throughout Scripture the promise is repeated: "I will make my dwelling among you. . . . And I will walk among you and will be your God, and you shall be my people" (Leviticus 26:11-12; see also Genesis 17:7; Exodus 6:7; Deuteronomy 29:10, 12-13; Jeremiah 24:7; 31:33; Ezekiel 36:25-28; Zechariah 8:7-8; John 1:14; 2 Corinthians 6:16; Hebrews 8:10; Revelation 21:1-3). *The covenant is relational.*

Paul was under the sentence of death from the emperor, but he was confident of the promise of life in Jesus. Paul's point is clear: the promise of life overrides all circumstances because God is a covenant-keeper. The promise was kept with "the appearing of our Savior Christ Jesus, who abolished death and brought life and immortality to light through the gospel" (2 Timothy 1:10).

Paul's reference to the triad of covenantal blessings—grace, mercy, and peace (1:2)—reminds us that *the covenant is compassionate.* John Calvin explains:

> The word *mercy*, which he employs here, is commonly left out by him in his ordinary salutations. I think that he introduced it, when he

poured out his feelings with more than ordinary vehemence. Moreover, he appears to have inverted the order; for, since "mercy" is the cause of "grace," it ought to have come before it in this passage. But still it is not unsuitable that it should be put after *grace*, in order to express more clearly what is the nature of that grace, and whence it proceeds; as if he had added, in the form of a declaration, that the reason why we are loved by God is that he is merciful. Yet this may also be explained as relating to God's daily benefits, which are so many testimonies of his "mercy"; for, whenever he assists us, whenever he delivers us from evils, pardons our sins, and bears with our weakness, he does so, because he has compassion on us.[5]

Paul continued to reinforce his covenantal emphasis by referring to his ancestors. This would have reminded Timothy that *the covenant is corporate.* You can feel a surge of confidence as Paul's thoughts meandered from Abraham to Timothy and as he identified with the company of the redeemed. When God bound Himself to us in covenant loyalty, He united us to His other children. We are connected to the community of believers throughout history and throughout the world. The church of Jesus Christ has triumphed and will triumph through the ages.

It is also noteworthy that Paul referred to Timothy's grandmother and mother. He acknowledged their ministry as a part of covenant continuity. He recognized the influence of a godly mother and grandmother in giving the gospel to the next generation. *The covenant is generational.**

The covenant should characterize all of church life. Consider these examples of how characteristics of the covenant will influence a women's ministry.

• *The covenant is sovereignly initiated:* When those in leadership have a strong trust in the sovereignty of God, they will trust Him to accomplish His purposes. He is the Sovereign King of His Church, and any desire to take control of people or plans is sin.

• *The covenant is restorative:* A women's ministry will be a restoring, reconciling gospel ministry when women understand that "God . . . through Christ reconciled us to himself and gave us the ministry of reconciliation . . . entrusting to us the message of reconciliation. Therefore, we are ambassadors for Christ, God making his appeal through us" (2 Corinthians 5:18-20).

• *The covenant is relational*: A women's ministry should teach women how to have covenant relationships that mirror God's relationship with us.

• *The covenant is compassionate*: A women's ministry should equip women to express our helper design through practical ministries of compassion.

• *The covenant is corporate*: A women's ministry should teach women that isolationism and independence are antithetical to the covenant way of life. Women should be taught to think biblically and live covenantally. They should be given opportunities to assume their corporate privileges and responsibilities in the covenant community.

• *The covenant is generational*: A women's ministry should equip women to pass the legacy of biblical womanhood to the next generation of women.

THE TASK

In light of the foundational truths woven throughout the Pastoral Letters, and the foundational truths of woman's design and calling, we have at least three tasks.

First, as we consider passages relating specifically to the role of women in the church, we must see them in light of these foundational truths. The brilliance and potency of a passage is not fully understood if it is unplugged from the whole of Scripture.

> **Without a proper esteem and love for Christ Himself, and an understanding of His covenant love for His church, we will lack the motive-force to serve Him in the world. If our ultimate motivation for service to God is simply because we love people, we will never be able to sustain the call to service that God has given to us because the very people we are called to serve will break our hearts. It is only the grace of Christ that enables us to persevere. (Ligon Duncan)**

Second, as we consider implications for women's ministry, we must vigilantly cling to these biblical truths. We must thoughtfully screen every plan and decision to be sure that it is a corollary of Scripture.

Third, above all, leaders of a women's ministry must pray for the women they lead. Pray that God will "open [their] eyes, that [they] may behold wondrous things out of [His] law" (Psalm 119:18).

THE TOOLS

The concepts in this chapter provide very practical guidelines for designing, planning, and evaluating a women's ministry.

Foundational Themes

The foundational themes of the Pastoral Letters—the gospel, truth, sound doctrine, discipleship, and covenant—should be core values of a women's ministry. Leaders of a women's ministry should continually and prayerfully discuss their commitment to these truths and evaluate the connection of every activity to them.

Characteristics of the Covenant

These characteristics provide a grid to study Scripture as well as helpful diagnostic questions for leadership training and event planning. For example:

• In a Bible study, ask women to identify characteristics of the covenant in a passage. This will help them to see the passage in light of the whole of Scripture.

• When training leaders, ask them to consider the responsibilities of their job description and then to identify characteristics of the covenant that can be exemplified as they execute those responsibilities. Women will be energized when they go beyond the functional value of their tasks and see the theological reasons. In one group, a young accountant who serves as the treasurer of their women's ministry became radiant when she exclaimed, "When I write thank you notes to those who make a contribution to the ministry, or who give a scholarship for someone to attend a retreat, I suppose I am nurturing community life among our women." She was immediately validated as others responded by sharing what her personalized handwritten notes had meant to them.

• When planning events, consider what characteristics of the covenant are driving the planning. How will community be nurtured among the women? (Perhaps you will have greeters, or a hostess at each table.) Will this event teach women about ministries of compassion? (Perhaps through a testimony from someone who was ministered to through meals during a time of illness or grief.) How will this event nurture relationships in the church? (Perhaps a panel of wives of elders can address questions such as: Why are you and your husband willing to spend so much time and energy serving our church? How can we pray for you and your family?)

Fanny Gomez, Reformed Baptist Iglesia Biblica del Señor Jesucristo Church, Santo Domingo, DOMINICAN REPUBLIC

The six pastors' wives of our church studied several of the *Biblical Foundations for Womanhood* books, and then we taught *The True Woman* in a Sunday school class for women. At the conclusion of the study we celebrated with a tea party. We asked several women to prepare tables using simple items that would help us know them better. It was a lovely time, but the best part was when we asked the women at each table to share what the study meant in their lives. Two of the testimonies at my table were particularly precious. A fifteen-year-old said, "I am thankful for the opportunity to learn about womanhood while I'm young. Now I understand that I can't wait until I am older to cultivate these virtues in my life." A sixteen-year-old said, "I learned so much, but two things were especially helpful. First, I never liked doing chores at home. I really disliked washing dishes and cleaning, but now my family is surprised because my attitude has changed. Now I understand that I need to cultivate domesticity in my life. I still don't like washing dishes, but now I do it with a different attitude. Also, having the experience of praying for an older lady and having her pray for me has been amazing."

Ninety women on an island in the Caribbean enjoyed true fellowship with one another, learned from one another, and shared testimonies that gave glory to God. What's next? The pastors' wives continue to study together and to meet with groups of women, we plan to repeat the class next year because many who did not take it have requested it, the principal of our church school asked me to teach *The True Woman* to ninth and tenth graders as a required course, and I had the privilege to go to Cuba and teach biblical womanhood to sisters in that country. When I returned home, I received a letter that included the following testimony from a woman who is a new Christian.

"The value and work given by God to the woman was discovered for me. I began to feel proud of being a woman and of the place my Lord destined for me in His creation."

Biblical Foundations for Womanhood resources that amplify concepts mentioned in this chapter:
- The content and context of biblical discipleship: *Heirs of the Covenant*, Chapters 1—2.
- A discipleship perspective of Titus 2:3-5: The *Legacy of Biblical Womanhood*, Chapter 4.
- A practical application of the covenant: *Heirs of the Covenant* and *Your Home a Place of Grace*.
- Characteristics of the covenant: *The Legacy of Biblical Womanhood*, pp. 202-205.
- Woman's creation design as a helper, and her redemptive calling to be a life-giver: *The Legacy of Biblical Womanhood*, Chapters 1—10.

NOTES:

1. R. B. Kuiper, *The Glorious Body of Christ* Grand Rapids, MI: Eerdmans, 1983), 91.

2. John Stott, *Guard the Truth* (Downers Grove, IL: InterVarsity Press, 1996), 201.

3. Ibid., 10.

4. Ibid., 186.

5. John Calvin, *Commentaries on The Epistles to Timothy, Titus and Philemon*, trans. William Pringle (Grand Rapids, MI: Baker Book House, 1981), 184.

5

1 Timothy 2:9–15 Submission

I love thy kingdom, Lord,
The house of thine abode,
The church our blest Redeemer saved
With his own precious blood.

TIMOTHY DWIGHT[1]

*I*n Chapter Two Ligon gave five reasons a women's ministry is important in every healthy evangelical church. I will repeat these reasons in Chapters Five through Nine, and then discuss biblical principles and practical applications to address these issues through a women's ministry.

Ligon's first reason is: Women's ministry is important because through it we have the opportunity to address helpfully the issue of the nature of manhood and womanhood—an issue that is very much at the heart of the cultural transition that we find ourselves in the midst of right now. Male/female role relationships, the definition of the family, homosexual rights—all of these are bellwether issues of our culture. Behind the shifts in our society's attitude toward these issues is a worldview megashift, moving from a Judeo-Christian or biblical framework to a pagan worldview. Until about 1970 we had been operating from the residue of a Christian worldview; since that time we have seen a dramatic and rapid shift to an essentially pagan worldview. Unfortunately, one way this pagan framework is being actively imported into the church by self-avowed Christian leaders is through their compromise on the subject of biblical manhood and womanhood. Bruce Ware, professor of theology at Southern Baptist Seminary, says:

> Today . . . the primary areas in which Christianity is pressured to conform are on issues of *gender* and *sexuality*. Postmoderns and ethical relativists care little about doctrinal truth claims; these seem to them innocuous, archaic, and irrelevant to life. What they *do* care about, and care with a vengeance, is whether their feminist agenda and sexual perversions are tolerated, endorsed and expanded in an increasingly neo-pagan landscape. Because this is what they care most about, it is precisely here that Christianity is most vulnerable. To lose the battle here is to subject the Church to increasing layers of departure from biblical faith. And surely, it will not be long until ethical departures (the Church yielding to feminist pressures for women's ordination, for example) will yield even more central doctrinal departures (questioning whether Scripture's inherent patriarchy renders it fundamentally untrustworthy, for example). I find it instructive that when Paul warns about departures from the faith in the latter days, he lists ethical compromises and the searing of the conscience as the prelude to a full-scale doctrinal apostasy (1 Tim 4:1-5).

Ethical compromise comes first, then the doctrinal sellout follows. We evangelicals care about doctrine. The cultural progressives don't. But if we capitulate to their ethical reordering, doctrinal unfaithfulness is certain to follow.

The text for this present chapter calls the church to adhere to the biblical teaching of male/female role relationships in the church. This goes to the very heart of the nature of manhood and womanhood.

THE TEXT: 1 TIMOTHY 2:9-15

> . . . *women should adorn themselves in respectable apparel, with modesty and self-control, not with braided hair and gold or pearls or costly attire, but with what is proper for women who profess godliness—with good*

works. Let a woman learn quietly with all submissiveness. I do not permit a woman to teach or to exercise authority over a man; rather, she is to remain quiet. For Adam was formed first, then Eve; and Adam was not deceived, but the woman was deceived and became a transgressor. Yet she will be saved through childbearing—if they continue in faith and love and holiness, with self-control.

I am fascinated by the fact that there are no aberrant ideas in Scripture. Every concept and event is interwoven to tell one glorious story. Everything that Scripture says about women is consistent with everything else Scripture says about everything else. What Scripture says about womanhood is part of the self-revelation of the Triune God and His relationship with His people. First Timothy 2:9-15 is no exception.

Another fascinating fact leaves me breathless: when you string together the passages in the Pastoral Letters that speak specifically to the issue of the role of women in the church, the mission and principles of a women's ministry materialize. Even the order of these passages unfolds a logical scope and sequence to develop a coherent apologetic for a women's ministry. Surely it is by design that submission is the first topic to be considered.

Finally, I am awestruck that Paul's polemic on submission is preceded by a tender assurance of God's sovereign love. "For there is one God, and there is one mediator between God and men, the man Christ Jesus, who gave himself as a ransom for all" (1 Timothy 2:5-6). The God-man who paid the ransom for my soul is the One who tells me how life is to be ordered in His Kingdom. Gratitude for such grace compels me to trust and obey.

Paul begins his tutorial with an outward manifestation of a submissive heart.

Appropriate Apparel

In Chapter 1 Paul warned Timothy about those who taught false doctrines and stirred up controversies. It is likely that the false teachers encouraged a display of wealth in worship. Paul's counterpoint is that "women should adorn themselves in respectable apparel." There should be a spirit of modesty and humility in our worship. An emphasis on outward adornment focuses a woman, as well as others, on herself rather than on the rightful Object of worship.

There is no virtue in being unfashionable. This is not a call to plainness. It is a call to a purity of heart that is reflected in our outward appearance.

Women of every age must be guided to maturity and sound judgment so that their outward adornment reflects an inner adornment of grace. The temptation to flaunt wealth and physical attributes did not end with the first century. Those who lead a women's ministry should have a sanctified sense of appropriateness. They should teach and model for other women a purity of heart that permeates every area of life.

Serious Study

Paul continues to build his case by inviting women to go beyond immature flamboyance to serious study of God's Word.

At first-read the words "Let a woman learn quietly . . ." sound condescending and constraining to a twenty-first-century woman, but to the recipients of this letter it was an innovative invitation to learn. John Stott explains that the women would have been "honoured by their responsibility to learn (11), in contrast to the chauvinistic Rabbinical opinion expressed in the Jerusalem Talmud that it would be better for the words of Torah to be burned, than that they should be entrusted to a woman."[2]

The word translated "quietly" is derived from the same word that is used in 1 Peter 3:4, where Peter speaks of "the imperishable beauty of a gentle and quiet spirit." This Greek word "indicates tranquility arising from within, causing no disturbance to others . . . it is associated with 'meek' and is to characterize the spirit or disposition."[3]* Inner tranquillity is a work of grace. It is the sanctified attitude of the serious student who has a teachable heart.

A women's ministry should be a quiet-spirited ministry that causes no disturbance to the male leadership. For it to be so, the leaders of a women's ministry should have teachable, humble spirits that are ready to listen and learn.

Ecclesiastical Submission

The directive "I do not permit a woman to teach or to exercise authority over a man" (v. 12) is not an attempt to demean women. The Greek word that is translated "authority" means judicial or governing authority; so it refers to the authoritative preaching of the Word. Paul is teaching a biblical ecclesiology that reflects the creation order, thus reflecting the character of God, thus reflecting the gospel.

Paul did not patronize women by pussyfooting around this issue. He gave them credit for understanding that submission has nothing to do with status. Submission is about function. Equality of being and differentiation of function characterize the Trinity. The Persons of the Godhead are "the same in substance, equal in power and glory,"[4] but each has a different function in the accomplishment of our salvation. Dr. Stott expounds this point:

> We should begin by affirming, against what is fashionable and "politically correct," that a woman's "submission" to "male authority" is in God's purpose normative. . . . Not that "authority" is to be understood in terms of decision-making, let alone the wielding of unlimited power. In Ephesians 5:21ff. . . . Paul interprets the husband's position as "head" of his wife as modeled on Christ being "head" of his church. And this is a caring not a crushing headship, a headship of self-sacrifice not self-assertion, of love not pride, intended to be liberating not enslaving. Nor is male headship incompatible with sexual equality, any more than the assertion that "the head of Christ is God" [1 Corinthians 11:3] is incompatible with the unity of the Father and the Son in the Godhead.[5]

This dictum is neither a reaction to nor accommodation of culture; it is grounded in the creation order. In Scripture firstness signifies authority. Headship and submission are God's ordained order for achieving oneness in marriage and unity in the church.*

Submission is not a legalistic list of behaviors. It is an attitude of the heart that believes God's kingdom order is good because we trust Him. It is a passion of the heart that loves "the church our blest Redeemer saved" more than self.

There are four things this passage does not do:

• This passage does not call women to submit to false teaching. "The Word of God, which is contained in the Scriptures of the Old and New Testaments, is the only rule to direct us how we may glorify and enjoy him."[6]

• This passage does not address male leadership in arenas other than the family and church. Pastor Kent Hughes explains:

> [I]t must be noted that these instructions have nothing directly to say about teaching and authority in the marketplace or the academy or the public square. They are about order in the church. Neither do these directives allow any man within the church, by virtue of his gender, to exercise authority over women in the church. Such more generally explicit authority only exists within the sacred covenant of marriage and family, and then it is only to be exercised with the self-giving spirit of Christ (cf. Ephesians 5:22-32).[7]

• Women are not instructed to submit to each individual elder. Biblical ecclesiology entrusts leadership to a body of elders. There is safety in this structure.

• Women are not told to submit to domineering, controlling, mean-spirited men. Immediately following this passage Paul gives the qualifications for elders. They are to be above reproach, sober-minded, self-controlled, respectable, not violent but gentle. They must be dignified, mature men who are well thought of even by those outside the church (3:1-7).

The passage does call women to put the priority of the gospel above self-interest. It calls us to have the same passion as "God our Savior, who desires all people to be saved and to come to the knowledge of the truth" (v. 4). It calls us to be like Jesus "who, though he was in the form of God, did not count equality with God a thing to be grasped, but made himself nothing, taking the form of a servant" (Philippians 2:6-7). Paul's letter to Timothy, including this passage, tells us "how one ought to behave in the household of God, which is the church of the living God, a pillar and buttress of truth" (3:15).

The context of 1 Timothy 2:9-15 is corporate worship. It does not refer to submission in marriage, though that principle is clearly taught throughout Scripture. However, submission in marriage and submission in the church cannot be separated. If a woman does not submit in her marriage, she will bring that rebellious attitude into the church. A leader of women, including single women, must have a respect for and commitment to God's kingdom order in the home and church.

A Captivating Conclusion

Paul concludes by pointing the church to woman's redemptive mission as a life-giver. "Yet she will be saved through childbearing—if they continue in faith and love and holiness, with self-control."

Obviously this does not mean that birthing children merits salvation. Such a notion would deny the clear scriptural teaching of justification by grace through faith. This intriguing verse is explained by Dr. George Knight:

> Paul brings the section addressed to women to a conclusion with a note of encouragement . . . and an emphasis on continued Christian faith and godliness. . . .
>
> Essentially two views have been followed [in reference to the word *saved*]. . . . The reference is to either (1) salvation in the spiritual sense or (2) salvation in the physical sense of preservation. Similarly, essentially two views have been taken [in reference to childbearing]. . . . It is a reference to either (1) the birth of Messiah or (2) childbearing in general. . . . The most likely understanding of this verse is that it refers to spiritual salvation through the birth of the Messiah . . . Furthermore, this understanding fits the flow of Paul's argument. He points out that Eve . . . brought herself into transgression by abandoning her role and taking on that of the man. But by fulfilling her role, difficult as it may be as a result of sin (Gn. 3:16), she gives birth to the Messiah, and thereby "she" . . . fulfilled, of course, in Mary . . . brings salvation into the world. . . . There is thus a transition from Eve . . . back to women in general . . . in this way the passage serves to show women the importance of their role and of carrying it out in an obedient way, the note on which the passage ends (. . . cf. Mary's words in Lk. 1:38).[8]

Regardless of whether a woman ever births a child, her capacity to give birth reflects her life-giving mission. Every redeemed woman is called to have a life-giving ministry in God's covenant family. This ministry is not limited to our biologically reproductive years. We can be "full of sap and green" and still "bear fruit in old age" as we declare to others that "the LORD is upright; he is my rock, and there is no unrighteousness in him" (Psalm 92:14-15).*

BIBLICAL EXAMPLES

Whenever the creation order is inverted, there is disorder, destruction, and death. When we tamper with this order, even a little, we become life-takers rather than life-givers. Ask Eve (Genesis 3), or Sarah (Genesis 16), or Rebekah (Genesis 27), or Miriam.

Most of us resonate with Miriam's story. We are so like her. When she was good she was very, very good; but when she was bad she was horrid.

After Miriam's brother led God's people out of Egypt, he led them in praising God for their deliverance.

> Then Moses and the people of Israel sang this song to the LORD, saying, "I will sing to the LORD, for he has triumphed gloriously; the horse and his rider he has thrown into the sea. . . ." (Exodus 15:1)

When Moses completed his song, Miriam "took a tambourine in her hand, and all the women went out after her with tambourines and dancing. And Miriam sang to them . . ." (vv. 20-21).

Miriam was a leader of women. They *all* followed her. Where did she lead them? What did she sing to them? She sang Moses' song verbatim (cf. vv. 1, 21). She did not add her own nuance. She taught the women to submit to Moses' leadership by connecting them to his teaching. This was a vulnerable time for the Jewish community. They could have become heady with the thrill of victory and freedom. Imagine the problems Miriam could have caused for Moses if she had used this opportunity to establish her own ministry and to encourage the newly-freed women to assert their rights. Miriam promoted order and unity by submitting to Moses' leadership. She is an example of female leadership at its finest. She was a life-giver to Moses and to this fledgling band of people.*

But somewhere along the way Miriam began to grasp equality. She and her brother Aaron "spoke against Moses because of the Cushite woman whom he had married. . . . And they said, 'Has the LORD indeed spoken only through Moses? Has he not spoken through us also?' And the LORD heard it" (Numbers 12:1-2). He always does. He always sees our rebellious hearts and hears our destructive words.

The Lord called Moses, Aaron, and Miriam to the tent of meeting. He appeared in a pillar of cloud and called Aaron and Miriam to come forward. He spoke to them about Moses. The story is riveting.

> "He is faithful in all my house. With him I speak mouth to mouth, clearly, and not in riddles, and he beholds the form of the LORD. Why then were you not afraid to speak against my servant Moses?" And the anger of the LORD was kindled against them, and he departed. When the cloud removed from over the tent, behold, Miriam was leprous, like snow. . . . And Aaron said to Moses, "Oh, my lord, do not punish us because we have done foolishly and have sinned. Let her not be as one dead, whose flesh is half eaten away when he comes out of his mother's womb." And Moses cried to the LORD, "O God, please heal her—please." But the LORD said to Moses . . . "Let her be shut outside the camp seven days, and after that she may be brought in again." So Miriam was shut outside the camp seven days, and the people did not set out on the march till Miriam was brought in again. (vv. 7-15).

Miriam's rebellion did not just affect her; the entire community was brought to a standstill as they waited. Imagine the fear and confusion her actions and her punishment caused among the women. In this instance, Miriam was a life-taker. But Miriam went from rebellion to reconciliation because her mediator pled her case: "O God, please heal her—please."*

Our Mediator does the same for us—and more. Our Mediator went outside the camp for us. "For the bodies of those animals whose blood is brought into the holy places by the high priest as a sacrifice for sin are burned outside the camp. So Jesus suffered outside the gate in order to sanctify the people through his own blood" (Hebrews 13:11-12). And He "is able to save to the uttermost those who draw near to God through him, since he always lives to make intercession for them" (Hebrews 7:25).

THE TASK

Submission is the watershed issue for a women's ministry. It determines whether we have a complementarian or egalitarian view of women in the church. It determines whether we have an integrative or independent ministry. The corporate application of this passage is that a women's ministry should be under the authority and oversight of the elders of the church. The leaders of a women's ministry should pray for submissive hearts and should lead women to support and submit to the male leadership of the church.

Sisters in Christ, I challenge you to regularly encourage your ministers and elders to be faithful to Scripture, especially in the areas that they are most afraid to touch. Frankly, one of those areas is male/female role relationships in the home and in the church. (Ligon Duncan)

Mature women should teach younger women that they have no reason to be threatened by male headship. When women fall into the trap of thinking that equality means sameness, the church is robbed of the helping, life-giving ministry God fashioned and redeemed us to fulfill. Submission does not restrain women. Submission frees us to accomplish our kingdom purpose.

Above all, women who lead women should pray for the women they lead. Pray that they will "submit [themselves] therefore to God [and] resist the devil" (James 4:7).

THE TOOLS

The concept of ecclesiastical submission helps us answer two of the fundamental questions of this book:

• Who is responsible for the women's ministry in a church?

• How does a women's ministry relate to the other ministries in the church?

Ultimately the elders are responsible for the women's ministry, just as they are responsible for the care and oversight of all ministries in the church. They are also responsible for how various ministries in the church relate to one another.

Practical tools for executing this oversight (these suggestions would also apply to other ministries such as children, youth, Sunday school, and men's ministry) include:

• The elders should be involved in the process of recruiting leaders for the women's ministry. Whether they appoint these women or ask for names to be submitted, the elders should have final approval of the women who will serve in a leadership capacity.

• Elders should provide a process for women to report their plans and proposals for oversight. One way to accomplish this, as well as to help various ministries interface with one another, is to have a committee coordinate all of the discipleship ministries of the church.* This committee would include a representative from each of the discipleship ministries such as the Sunday school, children, youth, men's ministry, women's ministry, small groups, and choirs. Study materials, plans, and schedules can be coordinated and reported to the elders. This also provides a way for each ministry to find ways to support other ministries. For example, the youth ministry may offer to provide child care for a women's outreach event, or the youth ministry and women's ministry may partner to plan activities for teenage girls.

• The leaders of a women's ministry should seek the advice of male leadership. They should submit all materials to be studied to the elders for oversight.

• The women's ministry should be diligent to keep elders informed. Written proposals explaining the purpose and strategy for events, retreats, and new ministries should be submitted with sufficient time for elders to consider the ideas.

• Whenever the elders determine that a proposal must be rejected, the leadership of the women's ministry should pray for submissive hearts. If the decision of the elders needs to be communicated to the women, the leadership of the women's ministry has the opportunity to promote unity by their gratitude for godly elders who consider the needs of the whole church.*

Donna Dobbs, *Director of Christian Education, First Presbyterian Church, Jackson, Mississippi*

I am a single woman with a seminary degree who has spent my adult life in vocational church work, and I serve in a church that is considered very traditional. Because of the long history of strong Teaching and Ruling Elders at our church, some people have the mistaken impression that it might be a difficult place for women to serve. In fact, I was warned of this potential when I was considering joining the staff. What I learned was quite different. I found that godly male leadership is sacrificial, protective, and honest, and that in that context women's ministry can flourish.

As Director of Christian Education, the women's ministry is one of my responsibilities. The role of women's ministry is to help accomplish the mission our pastor and elders have determined that God has for the church. We do not want two separate agendas—ours and theirs—so the key question that dictates the mission of women's ministry is: "How can we help you?" This question guides all of our decisions as we pray and plan for our women's ministry. The men may not always know how we can help simply because they have not spent time thinking in those terms. However, it is what we think about, and it is what we should think about. A true helper makes suggestions and volunteers service that the men may never have thought to ask us to do.

In the process I've discovered that submission in the structure of the church is one of the ways God encourages women to use their community-building gifts to connect one part of the body to another. For example, when you don't make decisions unilaterally, you must explain the rationale and details of your ministry plans to the governing committees, pastors, and officers of the church so that you can obtain their approval. This, in turn, educates them about what the women's ministry is trying to accomplish and builds bridges and support that would never have existed if you made independent decisions.

I have also discovered the benefits of protection and correction through submission. There have been many times when my bleeding heart would have led me into entanglements that were unwise, but the male leadership saw the problem and enacted a wiser plan that served people's interests better in the long run. Or sometimes the elders say "no," and that may be hard to take, but I have learned that God is just as present in the "nos" as in the "yeses." I have become grateful for "nos" as a sure sign of God's leading.

After nineteen happy, fulfilling years of life and service in our church, I can testify that God's plan for church life really does prove His wisdom and goodness.

Biblical Foundations for Womanhood resources that amplify concepts mentioned in this chapter:
- 1 Peter 3:4: *The Legacy of Biblical Womanhood*, pp. 51-53.
- Submission: *The True Woman*, Chapter 10; *The Legacy of Biblical Womanhood*, Chapter 1.
- Submission in marriage: *Your Home a Place of Grace*, Chapter 4; *The Legacy of Biblical Womanhood*, Chapter 8.
- Life-giver: *The Legacy of Biblical Womanhood*, Chapter 1.
- Miriam, Exodus 15: *The Legacy of Biblical Womanhood*, pp. 58-59.
- Miriam, Numbers 12: *The True Woman*, pp. 170-180.
- Christian Education Committee: *Heirs of the Covenant*, pp. 63-64, 183-184.
- Women encouraging unity: *Leadership for Women in the Church*, Chapter 8.

NOTES:

1. Timothy Dwight, "I Love Thy Kingdom, Lord," 1800, *Trinity Hymnal* (Atlanta: Great Commission Publications, 1990), #353.
2. John Stott, *Guard the Truth* (Downers Grove, IL: InterVarsity Press, 1996), 85.
3. W. E. Vine, *An Expository Dictionary of NT Words*, Vol. 3 (Old Tappan, NJ: Fleming H. Revell, 1940), 242.
4. *The Westminster Shorter Catechism* (Atlanta: Committee for Christian Education and Publications, 1990), Q. 6.
5. Stott, *Guard the Truth*, 79-80.
6. *The Westminster Shorter Catechism*, Q. 2.
7. R. Kent Hughes and Bryan Chapell, *1 & 2 Timothy and Titus: To Guard The Deposit* (Wheaton, IL: Crossway Books, 2000), 69.
8. George W. Knight, III, *The Pastoral Epistles*, The New International Greek Testament Commentary (Grand Rapids, MI: Eerdmans, 1992), 144-147.

1 Timothy 3:11—
Compassion

Jesus, with thy church abide,
Be her Savior, Lord, and Guide,
While on earth her faith is tried:
We beseech thee, hear us.

May she guide the poor and blind,
Seek the lost until she find,
And the brokenhearted bind:
We beseech thee, hear us.

THOMAS BENSON POLLOCK[1]

Ligon's second reason that a church should have a women's ministry is:

It is important that we have a deliberate, intentional ministry to women in the church because the Bible teaches so much and so clearly on manhood and womanhood. It is never, ever safe to act unbiblically or to ignore biblical teaching, and the Bible says so much about the way that men and women are to relate, especially in the home and in the church. A church that wants to be biblical, then, will want to make sure the women of the congregation embrace and implement this teaching. And there is no better way for us to discreetly and appropriately address those nitty-gritty issues than in the context of a women's ministry. Without in any way discounting the regular pulpit ministry of the church, we should recognize that there are certain matters more aptly addressed and applied in the context of a specific discipleship of women, whether in large groups, in small groups, or in situations of confidentiality, as women minister to women.

The text for this present chapter calls the church to equip women for, and involve them in, ministries of compassion.

THE TEXT: 1 TIMOTHY 3:11

Their wives likewise must be dignified, not slanderers, but sober-minded, faithful in all things.

There is debate about whether the proper translation of this verse is "women" or "wives." Dr. Dan Doriani explains:

> The root of this uncertainty is the Greek word *gyne*, which can mean either "woman" or "wife" (the comparable masculine noun can mean either "man" or "husband"). Thus we are unsure if 3:11 addresses deaconesses or deacons' wives. . . . The phrase may mean one of four things:
> First, the women may be part of the general order of deacons. . . .
> Second, the women are female deacons or deaconesses who correspond somehow to the male deacons. . . .
> The third option is that women are assistants to deacons, perhaps taking on duties that especially pertain to ministry to women. . . .
> The fourth option is that the women are indeed the wives of deacons. . . .
> In my judgment, options three and four are more probable than options one and two, and number four is most likely of all. But whichever view is correct, Paul anticipates that women will have a hand in diaconal work . . . the church will live well, even if we cannot finally resolve the proper interpretation of 1 Timothy 3:11, if we keep women deeply involved in diaconal work. . . . The main thing is that women whom God calls to care for the needy do the work and help others do the same.[2]

Whatever is the proper translation of *gyne*, the broader application is the involvement of women in ministries of caring. This text highlights the concept that our helper design equips us for ministries of compassion and challenges a women's ministry to prepare women to be "deeply involved in diaconal work."

Community and Compassion

Years ago, when I began studying what the Bible says about womanhood, I was intrigued with the concept of woman being created to be a helper. As I studied passages in the Old Testament that use the same Hebrew word (*ezer*), I was amazed to find that it often refers to God as our Helper. I began listing the ways God is our Helper (see the chart on page 35). One day as I shared what I was learning with a friend I heard myself say, "These words seem to fall into the two categories of community and compassion." We both knew that it was an *Aha!* moment. Community and compassion capsulize woman's helper ministry.* (This is not to suggest that women are the exclusive purveyors of compassion and community. It is simply saying that our helper design equips us for and draws us to a practical dimension of these ministries.)

I was also growing in my understanding of covenant and was thrilled to realize that community and compassion are characteristics of God's covenant of grace. Because God has adopted us as His children, we are in community with His other children. As we reflect His grace to one another, it will be a community of compassion. The more I merged the two ideas of woman's helper design and God's call for us to live covenantally, the more I was captivated by the realization that each idea strengthens the other and that if you disconnect them, you weaken both.

- To isolate womanhood from the remarkable reality of covenant diminishes God's design and calling for women.
- Failure to fulfill our design and calling diminishes the culture of covenant among God's people.*

You can imagine my delight when I strung together the passages in the Pastoral Letters that speak specifically to the role of women in the church and once again I saw the concepts of community and compassion. I was delighted but not surprised because all of God's Word corroborates all of God's Word. Every part is connected to and consistent with every other part.

Deacons' Wives

Immediately after explaining God's kingdom order of male headship (1 Timothy 2), Paul gives the qualifications for men who are in positions of leadership in the church. This is a tender assurance to women that God does not intend for us to be abused or misused by those He places in authority over us. Tucked into the list of qualifications for deacons is the text for this chapter: "Their wives likewise must be dignified, not slanderers, but sober-minded, faithful in all things" (3:11).

Dr. George Knight raises the question of why this list of qualifications for women is introduced at this point in the passage. He explains:

> [T]he answer would appear to be that they are in some way involved in the diaconal service that the [deacons] are called to perform . . . [these women] are urged to manifest the four characteristics listed there, not because all women in the church must manifest these characteristics, but because of a special role that these "women" in particular have that demands these characteristics.[3]

Because of the nature of diaconal ministries, these character qualities are essential. These women may be called upon to assist in situations involving very personal issues. They must be mature women who can keep confidences. They must handle these situations with dignity and faithfulness that grow out of faith in the power of the gospel.

This passage has implications for a women's ministry. The characteristics required of deacons' wives correlate with the characteristics of widows in 1 Timothy 5:9-10 and older women in Titus 2:3. The women's ministry should disciple all women to be "dignified, not slanderers, but sober-minded, faithful in all things." Deacons' wives may do this training, or they may be the ones who are discipled by other women. The covenant way is for women to train women to love their husbands, and then if their husbands are called to serve as leaders, these women will be ready to joyfully and wisely assist them in their diaconal work.

Diaconal Work

The office of deacon is one of service. The Greek word *diakonos* in its specialized usage refers to the office of deacon, but in general usage it means servant. It is the word used by Jesus in Matthew 20:

> But whoever would be great among you must be your servant, and whoever would be first among you must be your slave, even as the Son of Man came not to be served but to serve, and to give his life as a ransom for many. (vv. 26-28)

It is by serving one another that we become a community of compassion. *Community and compassion* is not an innovative slogan; this is the essence of covenant life. Andrew Geddes (1518-1586) was converted under the preaching of John Knox and served as a deacon in his church. *The Christian Almanac* gives the following description of his diaconal ministry:

> Taking his cue from the biblical injunction to faithfully demonstrate justice, mercy, and humility before God (Micah 6:8), he also utilized both the prominence of his office and the power of his influence as a force for effective social change. He helped to organize the famed "seasons of prayer" in cottages all across Scotland that so profoundly shaped the character of the times, he pioneered a ministry to rescue and care for abandoned and orphaned children . . . [he organized] the Parish Relief Leal, a voluntary mercy ministry that was duplicated in local churches throughout Scotland in the years to come. Emphasizing what he called "covenantal compassion" and "community conciliation," Geddes left a lasting legacy for his beloved homeland and many of the Reform movements that would so indelibly mark its history.[4]

Much diaconal ministry is a life-on-life ministry of covenantal compassion. When those who need care are female, wise elders and deacons realize that it is not good for them to do this work alone. The complementary blend of the male and female design and function is needed. It is imprudent and inappropriate for men to give the relational care needed by hurting women. Male leadership should enlist their wives, and other women, to administer this kind of care. A pastor of an inner-city church said that much of their diaconal ministry is to single mothers and that the deacons could not possibly carry out this part of their ministry without the assistance of the women's ministry. A woman's creation design equips and compels her to give this help.

WOMAN'S CREATION DESIGN

Consider again three of the passages that refer to God as our Helper.

> But you [God] do see, for you note mischief and vexation, that you may take it into your hands; to you the helpless commits himself; you have been the helper of the fatherless. (Psalm 10:14)

> For he delivers the needy when he calls, the poor and him who has no helper. He has pity on the weak and the needy, and saves the lives of the needy. From oppression and violence he redeems their life, and precious is their blood in his sight. (Psalm 72:12-14)

> . . . you, LORD, have helped me and comforted me. (Psalm 86:17)

A redeemed woman's sanctified female instincts cause her to "see" the troubled and grieving, even if they are suffering in silence. Her helper heart pities the weak and needy, and her helper hands find ways to rescue and comfort. She does not need an official position for this diaconal work. Functioning under the oversight of those who are in positions of leadership in God's church, she does what she was created to do.

An article in *The Psychological Review* reported on a study that illustrates what Scripture tells us about woman's helper design. Two female researchers at UCLA noticed that when women were stressed, "they came in, cleaned the lab, had coffee, and bonded," but when men were stressed "they holed up somewhere on their own." They immediately began researching this phenomenon. They were probably unaware that what they observed was simply behavior consistent with our creation design. The article continued:

A landmark UCLA study suggests that women respond to stress with a cascade of brain chemicals that cause us to make and maintain friendships with other women. It's a stunning find that has turned five decades of stress research—-most of it on men—-upside down.

Until this study was published, scientists generally believed that when people experience stress, they trigger a hormonal cascade that revs the body to either stand and fight or flee as fast as possible. . . . Now the researchers suspect that women have a larger behavioral repertoire than just "fight or flight" . . . it seems that when the hormone oxytocin is released as part of the stress responses in a woman, it buffers the "fight or flight" response and encourages her to tend children and gather with other women instead. When she actually engages in this tending or befriending, studies suggest that more oxytocin is released, which further counters stress and produces a calming effect. This calming response does not occur in men . . . because testosterone—-which men produce in high levels when they're under stress—-seems to reduce the effects of oxytocin. Estrogen . . . seems to enhance it.[5]

Our Creator fashioned us to produce this cascade of brain chemicals. Tending and befriending is not learned behavior; it is instinctive to who we are as women. But this capacity is suppressed and distorted by sin and by cultural conditioning. Tending and befriending will look different in different women. Some will sit and cry with a grieving widow; some will make funeral arrangements; some will clean her house. A culture of covenant will teach women the truth about womanhood and encourage them to unleash their life-giving capacity to serve God's people according to their skills and giftedness. However, the right thing done the wrong way is not right. A women's ministry should engage in ministries of compassion the covenant way.

THE RIGHT THING — THE RIGHT WAY

Ministries of compassion are a hallmark of biblical faith. It is usually easy to enlist Christian women to care about issues relating to the oppressed and afflicted, but a women's ministry must exercise wisdom and caution as we encourage women to become engaged in caring ministries. We must follow biblical principles. We will consider two of the principles that will help a women's ministry to do the right thing the right way.

Principle #1: Submission

This text is consistent with the principle of ecclesiastical submission in 1 Timothy 2:9-15. The kingdom order of male headship liberates women to fulfill their redemptive function. From the world's perspective, submission restrains women. From a gospel perspective, submission frees us to do what we have been created and redeemed to do.

Just as there are potential dangers when men are involved in some diaconal ministries without the assistance of women, it is equally risky for women to be involved in these ministries without the leadership and oversight of men. The risk is not that women are not capable; the risk is the lingering rebellion in our hearts against God's kingdom order.

Of course, this does not mean that an individual woman must ask for approval from the elders before she volunteers to work at a crisis pregnancy center or to take meals to the elderly, but it does mean that if she is married she should have her husband's support of her involvement in that ministry.

The point is, no matter how many bowls of soup we dish up at the soup kitchen, if we do it with rebellious hearts against those God has put in authority over us, it is not pleasing to Him.

Principle #2: Gratitude

Women should be continually reminded that ministries of compassion do not cause God to love us more. It is easy to fall into this trap of works-righteousness. Women will grow weary if they think that one more visit to a nursing home will earn more of God's acceptance and love. Covenantal compassion is a response of gratitude to the knowledge that God loves us as much now as He will love us for all eternity, not because we have merited His love, but because Jesus merited it for us. The more we know Jesus, the more energized we are by the grace of gratitude to show His loving-kindness to others.*

BIBLICAL EXAMPLE

The Gospel of Luke tells about an unlikely combination of people who accompanied Jesus as He "went on through cities and villages, proclaiming and bringing the good news of the kingdom of God" (Luke 8:1).

> *And the twelve were with him, and also some women who had been healed of evil spirits and infirmities: Mary, called Magdalene, from whom seven demons had gone out, and Joanna, the wife of Chuza, Herod's household manager, and Susanna, and many others, who provided for them out of their means. (vv. 2-3)*

Apparently there was no tension between the disciples and the women. This is remarkable since the disciples were called to the position of apostleship and the women were the ones providing for them out of their own means. This beautiful example of complementarianism freed these women to extend covenant mercy to one another. There is much to learn from them about the power of the gospel.

At a women's conference, Dr. Bryan Chapell, president of Covenant Theological Seminary, preached on this text. In his sermon entitled "When Women Care" he gave the following insights about the women who followed Jesus:

> One of those with Jesus was Mary Magdalene "from whom seven demons had come out" (v. 2). We do not know the consequences of Mary's possession. Long tradition in the church identifies her as an immoral woman, though there is no biblical proof for this. Unquestionably, however, one with seven demons was deeply troubled. For her to be with Jesus was no doubt to cause others to question, "What is Jesus doing with someone like her?" She was an outcast among outcasts. Her past, her reputation, her social status, her spiritual record were all reasons for even these rejected women to reject her. They did not.
>
> Jesus extended the benefits of the covenant without discrimination to this troubled woman, and in supporting His ministry, the other women did the same. . . .
>
> The questions that others had about Mary Magdalene's being with Jesus would have been nothing compared to the questions that had to

do with Joanna, identified as "the wife of Cuza, the manager of Herod's household" (v. 3). . . . This was a household known for cruelty, immorality and the betrayal of the Jewish nation, and Jesus allowed the wife of the manager of that household to know His love. These women were supporting ministry not only to the troubled, but also to the terrible. For us to love mercy means that this is required of us, too. The ministry of women is to love mercy, to delight in seeing the benefits of the covenant extend even to those whose actions have made them undeserving of anyone's love, including—and maybe especially—our own. . . .

Jesus allowed the troubled and the terrible, and one more to be with Him. She is named Susanna (v. 3). Her name means lily. That is all we know about her. She is totally unremarkable, without significance or note—just ordinary. But Jesus plants this humble flower along Scripture's path to teach us something very beautiful about what happens when we show mercy to others.

This ordinary woman, by participating in the ministry of Jesus to the troubled and terrible, walked with Him. What greater honor can there be, than to be able to walk with the Savior King who is our Redeeming Lord? One who by any other measure was humble becomes blessed in a special relationship with Him as she ministers to others. This is not true of her alone. Think of what you know not only about Susanna but also about these other women who used their means to further the ministry of Jesus. They did not just walk with Him on this day of public teaching. From among these women were those last at the Cross and first at the tomb. . . . At the events most momentous for all eternity, these women were the ones most present. By caring for His ministry to others these women saw suffering and knew sacrifice, but in doing so they entered into a more vital, real and near relationship with their Savior.

These observations stand on its head our common understanding of who benefits from the ministry of mercy. We easily focus on the good to the recipient of the mercy, but what this text makes clear is that the one who expresses mercy can be even more profoundly affected. Those who wade through the misery and suffering for Christ's sake walk close to things eternal. Though ordinary and otherwise without note, a person who subverts her interests to Christ's purposes— who humbles herself—gets to walk with Him, know Him intimately, and share His heartbeat. . . .

When the ethic of mercy is daily lived in your life, demonstrated before your children, exemplified to your grandchildren, and taught to your Sunday school charges, then the mercy of God will become part of the daily heartbeat of the church—not merely a program but a way of life. God has specially equipped women to express the tenderness of His heart . . . expressions of mercy alone are not the gospel. But through such expression even those claimed by the gospel know it better.[6]

This explains how some of these same women could witness the horror of the crucifixion and not be immobilized by despair and grief. They had walked with Jesus. He touched their misery with His mercy, and they became merciful. They acted on the basis of their knowledge of and relationship with Him. So early on Sunday morning, they gathered to befriend one another and to tend the One they loved.

> When the Sabbath was past, Mary Magdalene and Mary the mother of James and Salome bought spices, so that they might go and anoint him. And very early on the first day of the week, when the sun had risen, they went to the tomb. And they were saying to one another, "Who will roll away the stone for us from the entrance of the tomb?" And looking up, they saw that the stone had been rolled back—it was very large. And entering the tomb, they saw a young man sitting on the right side, dressed in a white robe, and they were alarmed. And he said to them, "Do not be alarmed. You seek Jesus of Nazareth, who was crucified. He has risen; he is not here. See the place where they laid him. But go, tell his disciples and Peter that he is going before you to Galilee. There you will see him, just as he told you (Mark 16:1-7).

Anointing the body was a sign of affection. These women were not oblivious to the obstacle in their way. They knew there was a stone that was too big for them to move, but they went anyway because they loved Jesus. And because they went, they experienced the reality of His resurrection.

We are to care for the Body of Christ because we love Him. Caring for hurting people will always require more strength and grace than we possess. There will always be obstacles that are too big for us to remove. But when we go anyway, because we love Jesus, we will know the reality of our Risen Savior removing those obstacles and shining the light of His countenance upon us. We will know the joy of His grace enabling us to minister beyond our own abilities.

THE TASK

Under the oversight of the elders, a women's ministry should be a corporate helper to the whole church. This requires an integrative approach where the women's ministry serves other ministries, including the deacons.

The only reliable motive for encouraging women's ministry in the local church is an insatiable longing to see the display of God's glory in the local church. (Ligon Duncan)

A women's ministry can "keep women deeply involved in diaconal work" by teaching them the theological reason for ministries of compassion and the practical benefits of their helper design.

Leaders of women should continually challenge women to ask the Holy Spirit to examine their motives for ministries of mercy. Are they seeking self-fulfillment or God's glory?

The touchstone of a women's ministry is whether women are quietly anointing the Body of Christ with covenantal compassion, and then moving out into their neighborhoods and communities with that same loving care. The number of women involved in Bible studies and special events does not necessarily measure the fruit of the ministry. Rather, one outcome of Bible studies and events should be that women are comforting the grieving, assisting widows with insurance forms, teaching single moms how to budget their money, helping young mothers with sick children, working in crisis pregnancy centers, and visiting the elderly.

A woman told me that she and two other women from their church took a meal to a single woman who was recovering from surgery. They took enough food to stay and have dinner with her. When they arrived, two coworkers of the woman were there, so they invited them to stay for dinner. My friend said they had a delightful time, and after dinner she suggested that they pray together. When the prayer time ended, the two coworkers were weeping. My friend was startled and asked if anything was wrong. They replied, "This was such a sweet time. We are sad because this would never have happened in our church. It would never occur to the women to do this."

It is indeed sad when women are not being encouraged and equipped to bring this rich dimension of practical compassion into the life of the church.

Above all, women who lead women must pray for the women they lead. Pray that "the Father of mercies and God of all comfort" will comfort them in all their affliction, "so that [they] may be able to comfort those who are in any affliction, with the comfort with which [they] are comforted" (2 Corinthians 1:3-4).

THE TOOLS

Administering covenantal compassion often requires difficult decisions. Should money or food be given to a single mother? What care and protection should be given to an abused woman? When deacons take care of the investigation of these issues and the allocation of money, women are freed to administer whatever relational care is determined appropriate. Some examples of ways a women's ministry can assist deacons include:

• Identify and train women specifically for the task of being helpers in diaconal ministries. These mature women could work along with deacons' wives to assist the deacons.

• Enlist women to be prayer supporters for those who are doing the hands-on work of ministering to wounded and hurting women.

• Provide classes and seminars for women who receive diaconal help. Often women who are in difficult situations need spiritual mothers to teach skills or provide child care.

• Coordinate the food ministry so meals can be provided for the sick or for a grieving family.

• Coordinate a helping-hands ministry to provide rides for the elderly to doctors' appointments, relief for a caregiver to be able to run errands, or help for a new mother.

• Develop the policies and procedures, including the necessary legal work, that may be needed for a mercy ministry.

• Develop a coordinated effort between the Bible study teachers and those responsible for ministries of compassion, so that all ministry tasks are supported with biblical principles. Tasks become tedious unless they are the product of sound theology.

• Ask the questions: How is the women's ministry anointing the Body of Christ? Does an ethic of compassion permeate the ministry of women in the church?

Dr. George Grant, Teaching Pastor, Christ Community Church, PCA, Franklin, Tennessee; president, Franklin Classical School; Author of THE MICAH MANDATE.

In 1824 the Glasgow Missionary Society founded the Lovedale mission station deep in the Cape Province of South Africa. The hardy Scots Presbyterians who staffed the station devoted themselves almost entirely to evangelistic work for nearly four decades. Alas, their sacrificial efforts bore little fruit all that time, and the Society was considering cutting their losses and closing Lovedale. In 1867, however, a young and ambitious Scottish educator, James Stewart (1831-1905) and his wife Mina Stewart (1841-1912), proposed turning the mission station into a mission school.

The Stewarts had arrived at Cape Town in South Africa some six years earlier in the company of Mary Livingstone, who was on her way back to the African Transvaal to join her pioneer missionary husband, David Livingstone. Like Livingstone, James believed he was called to help "open up" Africa's interior to the broader influences of Western civilization. Once that occurred, he was certain that commerce and Christianity would work hand-in-hand to end the evils of slave trading, tribal warfare, and primitive barbarism. After several wrenching false starts, he began to doubt that industry could succeed, and he was plunged into despair. Mina convinced him, however, that all was not lost. Perhaps, she suggested, before their dreams of indigenous development could be realized, the impoverished tribal peoples would have to be much more substantively trained, discipled, and educated. In order to run businesses, staff factories, and man industries, African men and women would have to be equipped and prepared. Mina urged James to consider mercy as a possible gateway to productivity.

Thus together James and Mina conceived of the idea of transforming the old failed mission station into a fully integrated institution of learning. The Stewarts were both products of a venerable Scottish Reformed tradition—an unswerving belief in the merits of education, hard work, and devotion to God. They became convinced that such a tradition, carried to the African peoples with grace, mercy, and compassion, might well prove to be the key to liberating Africa from the pagan bonds of oppression, ignorance, and brutality.

During their long and productive years of ministry, the Stewarts helped establish two other mission stations, a satellite school, and a fully equipped hospital—and they left a blueprint for a college, which was built after their deaths. James was lauded as the "educator to a race" and the "father of native African enterprise." More than a century afterward, Nelson Mandela hailed him as the "model Christian" and South Africa's "founder of freedom." Likewise, South African president Thabo Mbeki recently asserted that the impact on South Africa of Lovedale graduates was "incalculable in terms of helping us to get to where we are today."

Irrepressibly passionate but always gentle, stunningly brilliant but always accessible, racked by malaria but "compelled by the love of Christ," James Stewart was one of the most productive, effective, and tireless men in the history of missions. But he was always quick to point out that it was Mina who kept his vision clear. It was Mina who reminded him of the things that mattered most. It was Mina who enabled him to translate his soaring ideas into gentle and practical action. But then, for anyone who knows anything at all about church history that would come as no great surprise. Through the ages it has often been women who have helped their husbands and churches see the remarkable power of diaconal and mercy ministries to win hearts, change lives, and transform cultures. To perpetuate that great legacy may well be one of the most effective kingdom tasks that women in our day could ever undertake.

Biblical Foundations for Womanhood resources that amplify concepts mentioned in this chapter:

• Compassion: *The Legacy of Biblical Womanhood*, Chapter 7; *The True Woman*, Chapter 6.

• The relationship between covenant and woman's creation design: *The Legacy of Biblical Womanhood*, Chapter 2.

• The grace of gratitude: *The Legacy of Biblical Womanhood*, Chapter 5.

• Mark 16:1-7: *The Legacy of Biblical Womanhood*, pp. 22-23.

NOTES:

1. Thomas Benson Pollock, "Jesus, with Thy Church Abide," *Trinity Hymnal* (Atlanta: Great Commission Publications, 1990), #348.

2. Dan Doriani, *Women and Ministry* (Wheaton, IL: Crossway Books, 2003), 181-183.

3. George W. Knight, III, *The Pastoral Epistles*, The New International Greek Testament Commentary (Grand Rapids, MI: Eerdmans, 1992), 170-171.

4. George Grant and Gregory Wilbur, *The Christian Almanac* (Nashville: Cumberland House, 2000), 14.

5. S. E. Taylor, L. C. Klein, B. P. Lewis, T. L. Gruenewald, R. A. R. Gurung, and J. A. Updegraff, "Female Responses to Stress: Tend and Befriend, Not Fight or Flight," *Psychological Review* (2000), 107(3), 41-42. Cited in an Internet article by Joan Belden.

6. Bryan Chapell, sermon at the 1999 Women in the Church Conference, Presbyterian Church in America, Atlanta, GA.

7

1 Timothy 5 – Community

At home in my own house there is no warmth or vigor in me, but in the church when the multitude is gathered together, a fire is kindled in my heart and it breaks its way through.

MARTIN LUTHER[1]

Ligon's third reason that a church should have a women's ministry is:

Women's ministry is important because when biblical manhood and womanhood is denied or altered or unpracticed, it results in disasters for marriages, families, and churches. Unbiblical husband/wife relations can lead not only to marital failures, but to gender confusion in children and first-order societal problems. We see this everywhere today. Women's ministry provides a safe and secure environment where those kinds of things can be addressed. For instance, many marriages suffer continuous tension because the husband and wife lack an understanding of (or perhaps have a positive disagreement about) the biblical teaching on role relationships in the home. Women's ministry gives us a unique opportunity to grapple with these things in the kind of practical detail that will help the health and welfare of Christian marriages, and thus local churches.

The text for this chapter calls the church to nurture community life among God's covenant family. True covenant life will exemplify biblical manhood and womanhood in the home and church.

THE TEXT: 1 TIMOTHY 5:1-16

This text begins with a brilliant and succinct description of covenant community.

> *Do not rebuke an older man but encourage him as you would a father. Treat younger men like brothers, older women like mothers, younger women like sisters, in all purity. (vv.1-2)*

The covenant community is a family. Our relationships in God's family are not based on commonality of gene pool, geography, interests, age, or circumstances. They are based on grace—God's grace in adopting us into His family. Our commonality is rooted in our origin and our purpose. We have been born of His grace and redeemed for His glory. If anything less binds us together, the integrity of community life is compromised.*

Jesus' High-Priestly prayer gives the description and destiny of the covenant community.

> *Holy Father, keep them in your name, which you have given me, that they be one, even as we are one. . . . I do not ask for these only, but also for those who will believe in me through their word, that they may all be one, just as you, Father, are in me, and I in you, that they also may be in us, so that the world may believe that you have sent me. The glory that you have given me I have given to them, that they may be one even as we are one, I in them and you in me, that they may become perfectly one, so that the world may know that you sent me and loved them even as you loved me. Father, I desire that they also, whom you have given me, may be with me where I am, to see my glory that you have given me because you loved me before the foundation of the world. (John 17:11, 20-24)*

The Apostles' Creed affirms this union: "I believe in . . . the communion of the saints." Dr. R. C. Sproul explains:

This is referring to a holy fellowship, a *communio sanctorum*, that exists in the church of Christ. Indeed, it *is* the church of Christ. . . . Ultimately, the basis for Christian community is found in our unity with Christ. . . . But this communion does not stop with our individual union with Christ. The moment I enter union with Christ, I simultaneously enter a union with every person, living or dead, who also is in union with Christ. This unity of Christ's people exists and manifests the degree to which His High Priestly Prayer has been answered. This unity is no insignificant thing. Indeed, nothing can possibly separate us, for this unity and community are fixed by and in Christ Himself. This community is a heavenly community, but it also is a community in which we participate right here and right now—a unity that counts forever.[2]

Steve Schlissel, pastor of Messiah's Congregation in Brooklyn, New York, writes:

I admit it: I'm envious. I'm green when I look at observant ("orthodox") Jews. What do they have that we don't? Covenant consciousness: a way of thinking that begins with the assembly rather than the individual. There's an "us-ness" to orthodox Judaism that is missing from Western Christianity.[3]

The remainder of 1 Timothy 5 gives examples of the "us-ness" of true covenant life, and once again the lie that Scripture denigrates women is demolished with gospel truth. Paul's tutorial on covenant life begins with the care that should be given to widows. Caring for this at-risk segment of that culture was not a new notion. Scripture is replete with instructions about caring for widows.

For the LORD your God is God of gods and Lord of lords, the great, the mighty, and the awesome God, who is not partial and takes no bribe. He executes justice for the fatherless and the widow, and loves the sojourner, giving him food and clothing. (Deuteronomy 10:17-18)

God is the "Father of the fatherless and protector of widows" (Psalm 68:5). He "tears down the house of the proud but maintains the widow's boundaries" (Proverbs 15:25).

When Jesus entered the village of Nain and saw the funeral procession of the widow's son, "He had compassion on her and said to her, 'Do not weep.' Then he came up and touched the bier, and the bearers stood still. And he said, 'Young man, I say to you, arise.'" And the dead man sat up and began to speak, and Jesus gave him to his mother" (Luke 7:13-15).

And from the cross Jesus gave us the preeminent picture of covenant community.

> When Jesus saw his mother and the disciple whom he loved standing nearby, he said to his mother, "Woman, behold, your son!" Then he said to the disciple, "Behold, your mother!" And from that hour the disciple took her to his own home. (John 19:26-27)

The God of gods and Lord of lords, the One in whom there is no vulnerability, pities and cares for society's most vulnerable. It is His nature to do so; He can do no other. This care should be embodied in His church.

> He has told you, O man, what is good; and what does the LORD require of you but to do justice, and to love kindness, and to walk humbly with your God? (Micah:6:8)

> Religion that is pure and undefiled before God and the Father is this: to visit orphans and widows in their affliction, and to keep oneself unstained from the world. (James 1:27)

Ministry to Widows

> Honor widows who are truly widows. But if a widow has children or grandchildren, let them first learn to show godliness to their own household and to make some return to their parents, for this is pleasing in the sight of God. She who is truly a widow, left all alone, has set her hope on God and continues in supplications and prayers night and day, but she who is self-indulgent is dead even while she lives. Command these things as well, so that they may be without reproach. But if anyone does not provide for his relatives, and especially for members of

his household, he has denied the faith and is worse than an unbeliever.
(1 Timothy 5:3-8)

The Greek word translated *honor* includes respect and financial support. It is the covenant responsibility of the community to care for those women who have no family members and no means of support. This passage also underscores the responsibility of each family to care for its own.

The broader principle is that the church is to care for its members who are helpless and need assistance. Even when no financial support is needed, the vulnerable among us should receive the honor of loving care and respect. Pastor Kent Hughes writes:

> Today I believe the application of this passage should be wider, because modern American culture has produced a category of women virtually unknown in the first century—Christian women and children who have been abandoned by their spouses and left without family support. Godly single mothers are a new class of "widow." And those without family and resources are the church's sacred responsibility. Those believers who are involved in fleshing out our obligation are doing the work of God—true religion.[4]

Ministry of Widows

> *Let a widow be enrolled if she is not less than sixty years of age, having been the wife of one husband, and having a reputation for good works: if she has brought up children, has shown hospitality, has washed the feet of the saints, has cared for the afflicted, and has devoted herself to every good work. (vv. 9-10)*

Some commentators see two different, though overlapping, groups of widows. The first group (vv. 3-8) should receive support. The second group (vv. 9-10) should be "enrolled" because they have specific qualifications for ministry.

George Knight writes regarding the widows who are enrolled:

> The church commits itself to assist these widows and in turn may ask them to perform certain tasks as need arises. Noting all the dimensions of this arrangement keeps one from drawing the false conclusion that

the church does not help other widows who are either younger or who do not fully meet the requirements. But the passage does imply that the church enters into this permanent arrangement only with certain qualified widows and with mutually accepted commitments and possible responsibilities. Noting all the dimensions of the arrangement also guards against the erroneous conclusion that Paul is mandating a widows' organization in the church.[5]

John Stott also explains that this does not mandate an order of widows. However, he says that by the end of the second century "Tertullian gives us unequivocal evidence that an order of widows existed. In his time and in the third century the registered widows gave themselves to prayer, nursed the sick, cared for the orphans, visited Christians in prison, evangelized pagan women, and taught female converts in preparation for their baptism."[6]

A church may or may not have widows who need financial support, but every church needs older women who give themselves to prayer, nursing the sick, caring for orphans, visiting Christians in prison, evangelizing pagan women, and teaching female converts. This kind of ministry, and the requisite qualifications, is congruent with Titus 2:3-5.*

The qualifications for this kind of ministry are remarkable in our culture of professionalized and specialized ministry. These women were credentialed by their seniority (over sixty simply reflects the age after which it would be unlikely for a woman in that culture to remarry), marital faithfulness, and good works. The priority of marriage in this passage and in Titus 2 is significant. A husband should be the first recipient of a woman's capacity to show compassion and nourish community. If a woman bypasses her marriage, every other ministry will be polluted.

The examples of good works are equally noteworthy.

As examples Paul mentions what Newport White calls "commonplace duties," a selection which he regards as "characteristic of the sanity of apostolic Christianity." The first is *bringing up children*, meaning to "care for them physically and spiritually" . . . whether her own children or orphans. Secondly, *showing hospitality*, presumably to travelers, a quality specially necessary in presbyter-bishops and other leaders (3:2). Thirdly, *washing the feet of the saints*, a menial ministry usually reserved for slaves, but beautified by the example of Jesus (John 13:4ff.). Her fourth good work must be *helping those in trouble*, referring to any kind of affliction or distress, including persecution. After these four specifics Paul adds the more general expression *devoting herself to all kinds of good deeds* (10). Such an experience of humble, unselfish and costly service would qualify a registered widow to undertake similar ministries as an accredited church worker.[7]

The woman who qualified for this kind of ministry had a history of glorifying God in her "commonplace duties." She did not necessarily possess extraordinary abilities, but she demonstrated extraordinary faithfulness in ordinary life. Grace-engendered, commonplace duties, not dazzling programs and people, are the adhesive of covenant life. The *Westminster Confession of Faith* explains that those who are united to Jesus Christ are also "united to one another in love, they have communion in each other's gifts and graces, and are obliged to the performance of such duties, public and private, as do conduce to the mutual good, both in the inward and outward man."[8]

The characteristics that qualify women for this ministry are consistent with woman's design and calling as a helper and life-giver. The life-giving ministry of the third-century widows—prayer, caring for the sick and the orphans, visiting the oppressed, and evangelizing and discipling women—should epitomize the women's ministry in a local church. Women should be given opportunities to learn how to share their gifts and graces for the mutual good. The leaders of a women's ministry should have a biblical understanding of community life and should value the common duties. They should also understand and teach that good deeds are not just activities. Many women are in seasons of life or in situations where they are not able to spend time visiting the sick or helping those in trouble, but their decision to glorify God in their situation is a good deed.

Young Widows

But refuse to enroll younger widows, for when their passions draw them away from Christ, they desire to marry and so incur condemnation for having abandoned their former faith. Besides that, they learn to be idlers,

> going about from house to house, and not only idlers, but also gossips and
> busybodies, saying what they should not. So I would have younger widows
> marry, bear children, manage their households, and give the adversary no
> occasion for slander. For some have already strayed after Satan. If any
> believing woman has relatives who are widows, let her care for them. Let
> the church not be burdened, so that it may care for those who are really
> widows. (vv. 11-16)

In these verses Paul instructs younger widows to be engaged in the
self-sacrifice that is needed to care for a family. These are not heartless
commands; they are protection against youthful immaturity and a path-
way to spiritual maturity and ministry. Domestic duties are not a hin-
drance to sanctification; they are essentials of the common life. The
family is a context in which to develop godly character that will qualify
women for service beyond hearth and home. When love for Christ is the
matrix of domesticity, those duties become an aroma of Christ, the fra-
grance of life (2 Corinthians 2:15-16).*

When I was invited to go to the Czech Republic and Slovakia to
teach in women's conferences, my husband and I decided that it was time
to invite our thirteen-year-old granddaughter Mary Kate to be a part of
the team. We are committed to the principle of one generation teaching
the next generation, so we take others with us on mission trips. This time
we would be able to show and tell our own granddaughter about the
global reality of the covenant community.

Three weeks before the trip, Mary Kate's dad was diagnosed with
brain cancer. He was scheduled to begin treatment the same time we
were scheduled to leave. Gene and I knew that we could not leave our
family at this emotionally intense time. The others on the team did not
flinch. We had prayed and prepared, and they were ready. One even took
my notes and taught the material.

But what about Mary Kate? How do you tell a thirteen-year-old that
she will not get to go on a trip we had prayed, planned, and shopped for?
Finally I told her that we had prayed and decided it would be best if we
did not go since her mom, dad, and four siblings might need us. I was
not prepared for her response. She smiled. There was a sense of relief as
she said, "I have been thinking the same thing." In that moment I real-

ized that Mary Kate was beginning to learn the quiet peace and joy of simple obedience to Jesus. And it is obedience in the common duties of family life that will prepare her to one day tell women that God created us to be helpers and redeemed us to be life-givers in every situation and relationship, in every time, place, and culture. I pray that Gene and I will still have the privilege of taking Mary Kate on a mission trip, but I think that this time she learned something by not going. I know I did.

This passage does not exempt young women from serving beyond their families. A women's ministry should encourage all younger women to seek out older women who will teach them to serve others and who will help them learn to find the balance between ministry to family and ministry beyond family. Obviously this raises the practical question about single women, some of whom may like to be married but are not. The principles are still applicable. The church family provides opportunities for relationships with and service to people of all ages. Single women should not isolate themselves from the rich dimension of generational relationships and service that are needed in any church.

BIBLICAL EXAMPLE

The story of Dorcas is compelling. "Now there was in Joppa a disciple named Tabitha, which, translated, means Dorcas. She was full of good works and acts of charity" (Acts 9:36).

We don't know whether Dorcas was married, single, or widowed, but she understood the common life. She shared her gifts and graces for the mutual good. She is an exemplar of the qualifications listed in 1 Timothy 5.

When Dorcas died, two of the men in the church were dispatched to ask Peter to come "without delay."

So Peter rose and went with them. And when he arrived, they took him to the upper room. All the widows stood beside him weeping and showing tunics and other garments that Dorcas made while she was with them. But Peter put them all outside, and knelt down and prayed; and turning to the body he said, "Tabitha, arise." And she opened her eyes, and when she saw Peter she sat up. And he gave her his hand and raised her up. Then call-

ing the saints and widows, he presented her alive. And it became known throughout all Joppa, and many believed in the Lord. (vv. 39-42)

I love this story. Dorcas was not a high-profile personality. There is no mention of extraordinary giftedness. The passage simply identifies her as a disciple. Her union with Jesus united her to His people, so she served them in very ordinary ways. She made clothes for the widows. Perhaps she took meals to the sick and encouraged the young mothers. Whatever she did, her death left such a huge hole in that covenant community that two men were sent to fetch Peter. Surely other people in the congregation had died, but this death affected the heart and soul of the church. Personality-driven ministries may be impressive, but they don't bind hearts together. It is bound-together hearts that show the world that the Father sent Jesus and that He loves us.

THE TASK

The task is to think big—to think biblically.

Paul calls the church "the household of God." The local church is the family of God . . . when Paul used this familial language he was saying to Timothy, "I want you to realize when you look out on those people God has gathered that you are looking at the family He has chosen for Himself. Live and minister realizing that those people are God's kin." (Ligon Duncan)

The *Westminster Larger Catechism* helps us to think big thoughts with sweeping statements such as "The scriptures manifest themselves to be the word of God, by their majesty and purity; by the consent of all the parts, and the scope of the whole, which is to give all glory to God."[9]

As we begin to see that the "scope of the whole . . . is to give all glory to God," we will begin to comprehend the significance and agreement of each part. This is true of Scripture, and it is true of life. When God's glory is our overarching purpose, we begin to understand that every thought, word, and deed blends together to achieve that glorious purpose.

When leaders of women understand the grand consent between submission, compassion, and community, they will be able to disciple women to develop a "covenant consciousness." Submission, community, and compassion are inseparable parts of the whole of covenant life. Their synchronization is imperative for mature ministry. Covenantal community and compassion cannot exist in a vacuum of autonomy. It is within the authority structures ordained by God that we can experience the blessed oneness that our Savior prayed for us. Covenant compassion invigorates community. A community without compassion ceases to be a covenant community. This is applicable to all ministries, but the task of the women's ministry is to think big thoughts about the part of the church's ministry that is assigned to them—to see those parts from the perspective of "the scope of the whole, which is to give glory to God."

Another critical task for women's ministries today is to challenge older women to take up the mantle of Dorcas. The empty-nest years are not a time for self-indulgence for redeemed women. This is prime time to expand their horizons and to think about the scope of the whole. Then they will cherish each community-building task as part of the historical and global answer to Jesus' High-Priestly prayer for our unity. And then they will be able to disciple women to think biblically and live covenantally.

Above all, leaders of women must pray for the women they lead. Pray that they will be filled with wonder as they "see what kind of love the Father has given to us, that we should be called children of God" and that they will "love one another" (1 John 3:1, 11).

THE TOOLS

Nurturing community life in a congregation is much like developing family life in the home. We must spend time together. We must get to know one another. We must share a common life. There are endless ways that a women's ministry can breathe community life into a church. It begins by educating the women to have a covenant consciousness.

Language: Educate women by using covenant language. Hearing the language will help women wrap their minds and hearts around the covenant idea.* Use the characteristics of the covenant (see page 63) to plan events and activities. Develop a purpose statement for these activities, and use it in publicity and invitations. For example:

• All women and girls are invited to the women's ministry Spring Tea. The theme of this gathering is "Generation to Generation." The purpose is to strengthen our covenant community by telling the next generation of women about biblical womanhood. Each woman is asked to bring a tea cup with her name and a Scripture verse attached to exchange with another woman.

• Match women and girls, or older women and younger women, to exchange tea cups and prayer requests. Encourage the women to follow up by calling the girls or taking them to lunch. Have someone explain that the activity is not simply an exchange of tea cups, but an opportunity to obey the covenant principle of one generation telling the next generation "the glorious deeds of the LORD, and his might, and the wonders that he has done . . . which he commanded our fathers to teach to their children, that the next generation might know them, the children yet unborn, and arise and tell them to their children, so that they should set their hope in God and not forget the works of God but keep his commandments" (Psalm 78:4-7).

Stories: Provide opportunities for women to share their stories. Hearts will be knit together, and community life will deepen. For example:

• At the event above, ask two or three women to share the memories of a special tea cup. (Or, at Christmas, to share the memories of a tree ornament or a crèche.)

• At Bible studies, ask a different woman to share her story each week. You may even ask her to bring items that will help other women get to know her better (pictures, examples of her hobbies, books, or mementos).

Celebrations: Scripture tells us to "Rejoice with those who rejoice, weep with those who weep" (Romans 12:15).

• Baby showers and bridal showers, with a devotion and perhaps written prayers or words of encouragement to give the baby or bride, are wonderful ways to rejoice with those who rejoice.

• Celebrate graduations with a reception honoring the graduates. Ask each graduate to select someone other than a family member to give him/her a blessing or charge.

• Use a Women's Ministry Special Event to teach women how to weep with those who weep. Have a panel consisting of women who have been through various trials such as the death of a child, cancer, unemployment, divorce, or childhood abuse. Ask questions such as: How did women minister to you during this time? What are other things that would have been helpful? What did you learn about God through this experience? How can we pray for you?

*Encouragement:** Scripture tells us to "encourage one another" (1 Thessalonians 5:11).

• Host a luncheon for the senior saints.

• When the elders meet, surprise them with refreshments and a card expressing the gratitude of the women for their leadership.

• Deliver Christmas baskets to homebound members.

• Send care packages to college students and members in the military.

Enfolding: Scripture tells us to "Greet one another with the kiss of love" (1 Peter 5:14).

• Teach women to be intentional in enfolding the vulnerable, whether it is the newcomer who feels insecure, a single mom who feels alone, or the mother of a special-needs child who is unsure how her child will be accepted. Think creatively and strategically to plan ways to enfold and embrace everyone the Lord brings to your covenant community.

• Women with computer skills, and those with writing skills, could develop a web site and e-newsletter for women and/or for the church. Effective communication is essential for community life.

• Use special events to enfold women who are not a part of the women's ministry activities because of their commitment to serve in other ministries of the church. The goal is not to get every woman to participate in the women's ministry, but for the women's ministry to serve and encourage every woman in the church. Recognize the ministry of these women by asking some to be on a panel. Ask questions such as: How did God call you to this ministry? What has He taught you through this ministry? How can we pray for you and the ministry you are involved in?

The Leader's Guide for this book has many more ideas.

Women's Ministry in the Local Church

Pastor Ron Gleason, Grace Presbyterian Church, Yorba Linda, California
The congregation I serve desires to be a strong covenant community. Rejoicing with those who rejoice, weeping with those who weep, sharing each other's burdens, showing compassion and consideration, in good times and bad, and having the freedom to share our faith in Christ with one another binds us together in true fellowship.

Through the use of the ordinary means of grace, ordained by our Lord, men, women, and children grow into biblically mature Christians. The admonitions contained in Romans 12:15 ("Rejoice with those who rejoice, weep with those who weep") and Galatians 6:2 ("Bear one another's burdens, and so fulfill the law of Christ") are nourished and put into practice in our covenant family. The women in our church play a major role in the covenant life of our church. They stimulate relationships within our church, and they support the ministry of mercy in a variety of ways such as:

• planning "Families of Grace" functions and Sunday "Lunch Bunch" at the church after worship.

• participating in our small groups on Sunday.

• visiting new moms.

• writing cards of encouragement.

• welcoming members and prospective members into their homes.

• organizing prayer groups, prayer breakfasts, women's and marriage retreats.

• working with our covenant children during "park day."

• Women's Bible studies that are consistent with our doctrine.

• Titus 2 mentoring/discipleship.

These tasks may seem ordinary, but they are not. In an age when even Christians can be powerfully influenced by a worldly culture, the Church of Jesus Christ desperately needs godly women who pursue Christ, pursue holiness, and are willing to do whatever they can to build His kingdom. These graced women, led by the Spirit and the Word, are used by God to bless His church, their families, their neighborhoods, and in fact all of society. Covenant community occurs when ordinary men, women, and children serve and are transformed by the extraordinary God of Scripture.

Biblical Foundations for Womanhood resources that amplify concepts mentioned in this chapter:

- Community: *The True Woman*, Chapter 5; *The Legacy of Biblical Womanhood*, Chapters 2, 3, 4.
- Examples of the ministry of widows: Naomi to Ruth—*The Legacy of Biblical Womanhood* ; Anna to Mary—*By Design*.
- Domesticity: *The True Woman*, Chapter 9.
- Language of faith: *Heirs of the Covenant*, Chapter 6.
- Encouragement: *Treasures of Encouragement*.

NOTES:

1. Quoted in Robert G. Rayburn, *O Come, Let Us Worship* (Grand Rapids, MI: Baker, 1980), 30.
2. R. C. Sproul, "Bound For Glory," *Tabletalk* 23, No. 11 (November 1999): 4-7.
3. Steve Schlissel, "Covenant Community," *Tabletalk* 25, No. 9 (September 2001): 52.
4. R. Kent Hughes and Bryan Chapell, *1 & 2 Timothy and Titus: To Guard The Deposit* (Wheaton, IL: Crossway Books, 2000), 125-126.
5. George W. Knight, III, *The Pastoral Epistles*, The New International Greek Testament Commentary (Grand Rapids, MI: Eerdmans, 1992), 222-223.
6. John Stott, *Guard the Truth* (Downers Grove, IL: InterVarsity Press, 1996), 132-133.
7. Ibid., 133.
8. *Westminster Confession of Faith*, XXVI.1 (Atlanta: Committee for Christian Education & Publications, 1990), 85.
9. *Westminster Larger Catechism* (Atlanta: Committee for Christian Education & Publications, 1990), Q. 4.

Titus 2— Discipleship

[The church is] the Mother of all the godly . . . into whose bosom God is pleased to gather His sons, not only that they may be nourished by her help and ministry as long as they are infants and children, but also that they may be guided by her motherly care until they mature and at last reach the goal of faith.

JOHN CALVIN[1]

Ligon's fourth reason that a church should have a women's ministry is:

We ought to have an intentional, deliberate approach to female discipleship because men and women are different, and these differences need to be recognized, taken into account, and addressed in the course of Christian discipleship. This, as we have already noted, is something with which egalitarians cannot come helpfully to grips. The difference, the distinctness of men and women, is not only obviously displayed to us physiologically, biologically, and psychologically, it is written plainly for us on the opening pages of the Bible. When God created man, Moses tells us, He created them "male and female" (Genesis 1:27). Now this universal, creational reality has implications for discipleship.

It means that the distinction between male and female is something that is part of a human's (and especially a Christian's) being a bearer of the image of God. Think about it. Our God is one and yet eternally exists in three persons—Father, Son, and Holy Spirit. Our triune God is both equal and distinct, the archetype of the true individual and true community. Mankind, without living out the God-given distinction of male and female, relating to one another as God intended them to relate, cannot give adequate expression to this aspect of what it means to be created in the image of God. This truth needs to be explained and understood in the discipleship of the local church.

The universal, creational reality also means that our response to faithful biblical proclamation about God's design for male and female role relationships, and to the recognition of differences between men and women and how they work out in God's order for the home and church, should be *"Vive le difference!"* It's wonderful! This is not something to apologize for, nor something to be ashamed of in our postmodern culture, but rather this is the way God made us to be and live, and it's better than any other way. It is good. But it is so radically countercultural that it needs to be inculcated, specifically and explicitly, to men and women in the local church.

One way that these differences work out in the lives of Christian men and women is in the area of temptation. Men and women face different kinds of temptations differently. Thus the local church needs to address these distinctive temptations of men and women distinctively. And this is one purpose of intentional, deliberate ministry to women in the local congregation.

Of course, all of these points speak to the relevance of a distinctive discipleship of Christian men in the church, but they also indicate why we need to be self-conscious in our ministry to Christian women.

The text for this chapter calls the church to equip older women to disciple younger women.

THE TEXT: TITUS 2:3-5

Older women likewise are to be reverent in behavior, not slanderers or slaves to much wine. They are to teach what is good, and so train the young women to love their husbands and children, to be self-controlled, pure, working at home, kind, and submissive to their own husbands, that the word of God may not be reviled.

Since 1 Timothy and Titus were written about the same time and have similar purposes and themes, we will consider this text from Titus before looking at 2 Timothy, which was Paul's last letter. The chronological order of the texts that relate specifically to women is persuasive.

• 1 Timothy 2:9-15: ecclesiastical submission
• 1 Timothy 3:11: compassion
• 1 Timothy 5:1-16: community
• Titus 2:3-5: discipleship

Submission to authority is essential for covenantal compassion, community, and discipleship.

Discipleship that takes place within God's ordained authority structures and that includes equipping women for ministries of community and compassion will invigorate women and the church.

To disconnect Titus 2:3-5 from an understanding of biblical discipleship will reduce this amazing concept to anemic relationships and legalistic behaviorism. We must not take such a minimalist approach to such a magnificent mission. This text is one part of Paul's strategy for the discipleship, or Christian education, of a congregation. He challenges Titus, and the church in all ages, to guard the truth by equipping the people to show and tell truth to the next generation. This is not a new strategy. Throughout the Old Testament God's people were told the same thing.

> *Hear, O Israel: The Lord our God, the Lord is one. You shall love the Lord your God with all your heart and with all your soul and with all your might. And these words that I command you today shall be on your heart. You shall teach them diligently to your children, and shall talk of them when you sit in your house, and when you walk by the way, and when you lie down, and when you rise. (Deuteronomy 6:4-7)*

> *Give ear, O my people, to my teaching; incline your ears to the words of my mouth! I will open my mouth in a parable; I will utter dark sayings from of old, things that we have heard and known, that our fathers have told us. We will not hide them from their children, but tell to the coming generation*

the glorious deeds of the LORD, *and his might, and the wonders that he has done. He established a testimony in Jacob and appointed a law in Israel, which he commanded our fathers to teach to their children, that the next generation might know them, the children yet unborn, and arise and tell them to their children, so that they should set their hope in God and not forget the works of God, but keep his commandments. (Psalm 78:1-7)*

Psalm 78 then records stories of the past. Most of the stories are of the forgetfulness and faithlessness of God's children, some are of repentance and restoration, but all are of God's faithfulness to His character and promises because He never changes and His promises never fail. Telling the next generation about the past gives hope for the future because it assures them that God is a covenant-keeper.

Jesus confirmed and enlarged this strategy in His final commission to His church:

All authority in heaven and on earth has been given to me. Go therefore and make disciples of all nations, baptizing them in the name of the Father and of the Son and of the Holy Spirit, teaching them to observe all that I have commanded you. And behold, I am with you always, to the end of the age. (Matthew 28:18-20)

Titus 2 shows how a local church is to disciple God's people—by teaching them to obey all that Jesus commanded. The chapter begins and ends with an emphasis on teaching.

Teach what accords with sound doctrine. . . . Declare these things. . . . (vv. 1, 15)

Some of the principles of discipleship embedded in this amazing chapter will help us understand the specific directive to women in verses 3-5.

PRINCIPLE #1: ECCLESIASTICAL AUTHORITY AND RESPONSIBILITY

In verse 1 Paul addresses his instructions on discipleship to Titus, the pastor. The discipleship of God's people should flow out of and be consistent with the pulpit ministry. A biblical doctrine of the church is essential for biblical discipleship. As Ligon explained in Chapter Three:

> Paul refers to the church as "a pillar and buttress of truth." The church is the essential vehicle of evangelism and discipleship and the defender of the faith. The privilege of preserving and propagating the gospel was entrusted to the church by Jesus when He said, "All authority in heaven and on earth has been given to me. Go therefore and make disciples of all nations, baptizing them . . ." (Matthew 28:18-19). One of the things this means is that discipleship is to take place in the local church because that is where you baptize. The local congregation is where the truth is communicated to the next generation. The local church is where God especially meets with his people in the new-covenant era, and it is the essential instrument through which He propagates the truth.

Principle #2: Teach Sound Doctrine

In verse 1 Paul instructs Titus to "teach what accords with sound doctrine."

> This compressed phrase indicates that two strands are to be interwoven in Titus' teaching. On the one hand there is "the sound doctrine.". . . On the other hand, there are "the things which fit it", namely the ethical duties which the sound doctrine demands. . . . For there is an indissoluble connection between Christian doctrine and Christian duty, between theology and ethics.[2]

Sound doctrine systematizes Scripture so that we begin to see "the scope of the whole"[3] and the interrelatedness of each part. The result is that the disciple can think in biblical categories about all of life. In "Making Kingdom Disciples" Dr. Charles Dunahoo explains:

> The primary objectives of the kingdom approach of disciple making include knowing, understanding, and applying God's Word to all of life. . . . The kingdom model does not separate faith and life (as though such were possible). It focuses on integrating God's truth into all areas of life, and because of that, it is not merely an academic, information, or intellectual concept. The kingdom model applies to, serves, and ministers to all areas.[4]

We are products of our theology. What we believe about God shows up every day in every situation and relationship. Disciples must be taught all that Jesus commanded. They must be taught to see Him in all of Scripture. This demands a systematic, integrated, comprehensive plan for the discipleship of God's people.*

PRINCIPLE #3: THE COMMUNION OF THE SAINTS

In verses 2-10 Paul mentions six categories of people that reflect the profile of that congregation. To his emphasis on teaching he adds two other essentials of discipleship: relationships and application of truth to the dailiness of life.

> *Teach the older men to be temperate, worthy of respect, self-controlled, and sound in faith, in love and in endurance. Likewise, teach the older women to be reverent in the way they live, not to be slanderers or addicted to much wine, but to teach what is good. Then they can train the younger women to love their husbands and children, to be self-controlled and pure, to be busy at home, to be kind, and to be subject to their husbands, so that no one will malign the word of God. Similarly, encourage the young men to be self-controlled. In everything set them an example by doing what is good. In your teaching show integrity, seriousness and soundness of speech that cannot be condemned, so that those who oppose you may be ashamed because they have nothing bad to say about us. Teach slaves to be subject to their masters in everything, to try to please them, not to talk back to them, and not to steal from them, but to show that they can be fully trusted, so that in every way they will make the teaching about God our Savior attractive.* (NIV)

The simplicity of this plan is profound. Truth is to be taught in the context of relationships. This is not just the responsibility of the pastor. The communion of the saints is not just a cerebral concept. Every member has responsibility for every other member.

Older men and women have the generational responsibility to share their gifts and graces with younger men and women. They are to tell the stories of their failures as well as their victories, but that through it all God "divided the sea and let them pass through it . . . opened the doors of heaven, and he rained down on them manna to eat . . . he, being compassionate, atoned for their iniquity and did not destroy them. . . . He remembered that they were but flesh . . . he led out his people like sheep and guided them in the wilderness like a flock. He led them in safety, so that they were not afraid . . . he brought them to his holy land" (Psalm 78:13, 23-24, 38-39, 52-54).

Dr. George Grant has said, "A sense of legacy gives a sense of destiny."[5] The older generation can give a rootedness to the past that provides sturdiness for the future.

Who is the older generation? It is relative. A thirty-year-old has a generational responsibility to tell a teen about the faithfulness of God and to show her how Scripture is to be applied to life even as she learns from a fifty-year-old who is learning from an eighty-year-old.

PRINCIPLE #4: THE GOSPEL HAS A REDEMPTIVE, TRANSFORMING INFLUENCE IN BELIEVERS' LIVES

Verses 2-10 also give examples of what happens when sound doctrine is taught in the context of relationships that authenticate the doctrine. As truth moves out into life, older women develop a reverent love for God, young women become lovers of husbands and children, young men become self-controlled and mature, and slaves become trustworthy. This kind of growth in the grace and knowledge of Jesus develops individual and community maturity in Christ.

PRINCIPLE #5: THE GOSPEL HAS A REDEMPTIVE, TRANSFORMING INFLUENCE ON CULTURE

In some mysterious way, God uses the obedience of His people to have an amazing effect on the watching world. When women live out their life-giving calling, the world will not "revile" the Word of God (v. 5). The obedience of men leaves the world speechless—even enemies of the gospel are ashamed, "having nothing evil to say about us" (v. 8). And those in the most vulnerable positions in society are entrusted with the privilege of making "the teaching about God our Savior attractive" to those in authority over them (v. 10, NIV).

Cultural transformation happens in our homes, neighborhoods, and communities when God's people love Him and love each other and face the world with His truth and love. This is a remarkable chapter in which sound teaching and sound ethics coalesce into a beautiful picture of covenant life, which has a redemptive influence on culture. This is exactly what Jesus prayed for us:

> *The glory that you have given me I have given to them, that they may be one even as we are one, I in them and you in me, that they may become perfectly one, so that the world may know that you sent me and loved them even as you loved me. (John 17:22-23)*

PRINCIPLE #6: THE GOSPEL IS THE MOTIVATION

There are costly challenges in this chapter. Investing in the lives of others costs energy and time. It means taking relational risks. Why should we live so sacrificially?

> *For the grace of God that brings salvation has appeared to all men. It teaches us to say "No" to ungodliness and worldly passions, and to live self-controlled, upright and godly lives in this present age, while we wait for the blessed hope—the glorious appearing of our great God and Savior, Jesus Christ. (vv. 11-13, NIV)*

Christ came, and He is coming back. He appeared in grace as a baby, and He will come in glory as the King because He loves us. Our love for Christ is unpredictable; His love for us is unchangeable. It is gospel love that propels our obedience.

> *For the love of Christ controls us, because we have concluded this: that one has died for all, therefore all have died; and he died for all, that those who live might no longer live for themselves but for him who for their sake died and was raised. (2 Corinthians 5:14-15)*

PRINCIPLE #7: THE GOSPEL IS THE UNIFYING, INTEGRATIVE FACTOR

Paul concludes with an electrifying reminder of our unity in Christ:

[Jesus] gave himself for us to redeem us from all lawlessness and to purify
for himself a people for his own possession who are zealous for good works.
(Titus 2:14)

This is not individualistic language. Some discipleship is age and
gender specific, but no discipleship is separate from the whole. It all
blends together into a harmonious, interrelated system of educating
God's people to obey all that Jesus commanded. This is more than good
educational procedure; it is an expression of our redemption in Christ.
We are His purified people. Covenant consciousness will protect us from
the sin of being territorial about the portion of a ministry entrusted to
us. Covenant consciousness will cause us to think about the common
good rather than individual preference.

Biblical discipleship is not simply imparting facts or inculcating
personal habits of Bible study, prayer, and evangelism, as helpful as
those disciplines are. It is transmitting a way of thinking and living that
unites all the parts into the glorious whole of glorifying God. It is pass-
ing on a legacy of biblical faith and life to the next generation. It is the
impulse of our union with Christ. It is part and parcel of the covenant
way. It is not optional. Women discipling women is one part of this
strategy. The church is not to entrust this mission to just any women.
"Older women likewise are to be reverent in behavior, not slanderers
or slaves to much wine . . ." (v. 3). Women who disciple women are to
have a holy reverence for God that is reflected in their character and
conduct.

> The Greek word for "reverent" is *hieroprepes*, which occurs only here
> in the New Testament. It can mean either "befitting a holy person or
> thing" or more particularly "like a priest(ess)." . . . Or, as we might say,
> they are to "practice the presence of God" and to allow their sense of
> his presence to permeate their whole lives. . . . There is a great need in
> every congregation for the ministry of mature women, whom *The Book
> of Common Prayer* calls "holy and godly matrons." They can share their
> wisdom and experience with the rising generation, prepare brides for
> their wedding, and later advise them about parenthood.[6]

"They [older women] are to teach what is good, and so train the young women" (vv. 3-4).

> The Greek word translated train is *sophronizo*. It means "to cause to be of sound mind, to recall to one's senses" . . . the training would involve the cultivation of sound judgment and prudence . . . it suggests the exercise of that self-restraint that governs all passions and desires, enabling the believer to be conformed to the mind of Christ.[7]

Dr. Bryan Chapell makes pertinent observations about this passage:

> The simplicity of this plan may cause its profundity to escape those of us in modern society. For the ancient world this was a very bold plan. For a man to teach women to instruct others broke societal barriers and elevated the status of these women. . . . At the same time that he gives mature women new responsibilities, Paul places a constraint on the teaching of male leaders. . . . At least two observations should be made about this pattern. First, Paul's words again affirm the importance of community contribution for mature Christians. The older women are not to hoard their knowledge but rather should pass it on to younger women who need the advice of those with greater experience. Second, Paul does not tell Titus to teach the young women. This non-instruction probably reflects Paul's concern that a young woman perceive her husband as the male who is her primary spiritual instructor (cf. 1 Corinthians 14:35). Paul also apparently desires to establish a pattern of instruction in the church that does not lead to sexual temptation.[8]

Godly women who have embraced the truth of God's creation design and redemptive calling for women are called to train other women to think and live according to biblical principles of womanhood. This is the kind of life-on-life discipleship that guides and nurtures to maturity. It is a mothering ministry.*

BIBLICAL EXAMPLE

Two high points of human history were announced by an angel:

And behold, you will conceive in your womb and bear a son, and you shall call his name Jesus. He will be great and will be called the Son of the Most High. And the Lord God will give to him the throne of his father David, and he will reign over the house of Jacob forever, and of his kingdom there will be no end. (Luke 1:31-33)

He is not here, but has risen. (Luke 24:6)

Both announcements were given to women—and one was a teenager.

The profoundly beautiful and simple story of Mary puts into motion characteristics of the covenant, principles of biblical womanhood and women's ministry in the church, and principles of discipleship. It includes one of the most stunning examples of an older and younger woman in Scripture.

The angel's opening words to Mary reminded her of God's sovereign initiative: "Greetings, O favored one, the Lord is with you!" (Luke 1:28). The term translated "favored one" means that she was full of grace. It indicates that she was the recipient, not the source, of grace.

The humble obedience of Mary's response is praiseworthy, but it must be understood in light of the significant teaching moment that preceded her response. When she asked, "How will this be, since I am a virgin?" the angel answered, "The Holy Spirit will come upon you, and the power of the Most High will overshadow you; therefore the child to be born will be called holy—the Son of God" (vv. 34-35). It was then that Mary said, "Behold, I am the servant of the Lord; let it be to me according to your word" (v. 38).

The more we understand God's sovereign love, the more we gratefully submit to His authority. It is sovereign grace that empowers and compels us to be women who live under the authority of God's Word.

Mary had a covenant consciousness. She understood the communion of the saints. She knew her responsibility and privilege to be trained by an older woman. "Mary arose and went with haste into the hill country, to a town in Judah, and she entered the house of Zechariah and greeted Elizabeth" (vv. 39-40).

From the moment Mary arrived, Elizabeth was intentional in her discipleship of this young woman, and she had the one essential resource needed for the task: "Elizabeth was filled with the Holy Spirit" (v. 41). Elizabeth spoke words of welcome, affirmation, encouragement, and instruction to Mary.

> *Blessed are you among women, and blessed is the fruit of your womb! And why is this granted to me that the mother of my Lord should come to me? For behold, when the sound of your greeting came to my ears, the baby in my womb leaped for joy. And blessed is she who believed that there would be a fulfillment of what was spoken to her from the Lord. (vv. 42-45)*

Elizabeth's home was a safe place, and her words were life-giving for Mary. Mary was encouraged and equipped to glorify God. That is the essence of biblical discipleship. The results of Mary's Christian education are evidenced in her beautiful song of praise, the *Magnificat*.

She knew God's sovereign initiative in her life: "My soul magnifies the Lord, and my spirit rejoices in God my Savior, for he has looked on the humble estate of his servant" (vv. 47-48).

She had a generational perspective: "For behold, from now on all generations will call me blessed; for he who is mighty has done great things for me, and holy is his name" (vv. 48-49).

The next verses show a mature understanding of God's concern for and compassion to the poor and weak. She had a strong sense of covenantal community and compassion.

> *And his mercy is for those who fear him from generation to generation. He has shown strength with his arm; he has scattered the proud in the thoughts of their hearts; he has brought down the mighty from their thrones and exalted those of humble estate; he has filled the hungry with good things, and the rich he has sent empty away. (vv. 50-53)*

The song concludes with the prevailing theme of Scripture and of all history—God's covenant loyalty to His people: "He has helped his servant Israel, in remembrance of his mercy, as he spoke to our fathers, to Abraham and to his offspring forever" (vv. 54-55).

The Sovereign of heaven and earth, the Covenant-Maker and

Covenant-Keeper, not only chose this young woman to be the life-giver to the Life and Light of the world, but He prepared and positioned another woman to love and nurture her. Elizabeth gave Mary a sense of legacy, and Mary fulfilled her destiny.

THE TASK

Titus 2 gives legitimacy and limitations to a women's ministry. There is an unmistakable mandate for women to train women, but the extent of this training is somewhat limited. There are many times and places in church life where men and women study and serve side by side, but a primary task of the women's ministry is to train women in the biblical principles and practices of womanhood. This does not mean that biblical womanhood is the only thing that women study, but it does mean that there should be a resolute commitment to weave these principles throughout the entire women's ministry.

We need to help Christian women appreciate the manifold areas of service that are open to them in the church and to equip them distinctively as women to fulfill their ministry. But this will never happen if our approach to discipleship in the church is androgynous—that is, if it refuses to take into account the gender distinctives of the disciple. (Ligon Duncan)

Another task of a women's ministry is to emphasize that the Titus concept does not just apply to married women. All women are called to encourage and equip other women to glorify God by being helpers and life-givers. A woman does not have to be married and have children to know God's principles for womanhood and to help other women obey these principles.

The leaders of a women's ministry must be unyielding in their commitment to the principles of discipleship presented in Titus 2. They must be equally diligent in calling and equipping women to assume their generational responsibility to learn from older women and to train younger women. Whether women are teaching a women's Bible study or a class of teenage girls, chairing a women's retreat committee or singing in the choir, decorating for a women's outreach event or serving on the church's mission committee, they should be intentionally training or learning from other women. Women discipling women is not just a program—it is the covenant lifestyle of redeemed women. And it is the responsibility of the women's ministry to equip them for this mission. Someone is teaching women principles of womanhood. Is it the church or the world?

Above all, leaders of women must pray for the women they lead. Pray that God will raise up a generation of women who will declare, "O God, from my youth you have taught me, and I still proclaim your wondrous deeds. So even to old age and gray hairs, O God, do not forsake me, until I proclaim your might to another generation" (Psalm 71:17-18).

THE TOOLS

A women's ministry can begin by asking some strategic questions:

• How is the women's ministry enabling our church to obey Titus 2:3-5?

• How does our discipleship ministry reflect the principles of discipleship in Titus 2?

• How are women being equipped to train younger women in biblical principles of womanhood?

• What opportunities are women provided to develop nurturing relationships with older and younger women?

• Do we need an organized Titus 2 ministry?

If a Titus 2 discipleship ministry is needed, the women's ministry should work with church leadership to determine how this will fit into the overall discipleship strategy of the church. Some possibilities are:

• If there are large women's Bible studies, you may want to add a component where women are divided into small groups with a Titus 2 leader. These groups could meet before or after the Bible study to discuss application of the Bible study and biblical principles of womanhood.

• If a church is divided into small groups led by couples, the wife may be asked to learn the principles of biblical womanhood and to weave these principles into group discussions. She may also meet periodically with the women, or suggest they read books on biblical womanhood and share a summary at a group meeting.

• The women's ministry may determine a need to add a Titus 2 ministry to the existing ministries. See Appendix 2 for an example of how one church did this.

———————————————

Dr. Peter Jones, professor of New Testament at Westminster Seminary in Escondido, California, author of THE GNOSTIC EMPIRE STRIKES BACK *and* CRACKING DA VINCI'S CODE

Many in our churches continue to avoid the issue of gender because, they say, it is not a "confessional issue." All I can say is that gender is *the* major issue in the "confession" of neo-paganism. We can no longer keep silent. We must present the Bible's view of gender as an essential part of the coherence of the Bible's entire worldview, over against the "coherence" of the feministic, pagan agenda.

Let's be realistic. This pagan agenda has taken over our culture. Feminists and intellectual neo-pagans in control of the Academy and the media are working to eliminate any vestiges of patriarchy and normative heterosexuality. At the same time, they are seeking to institutionalize "pan-sexuality" for the coming brave new world, where all gender choices are normative. At a popular level, on virtually every other page of the wildly successful novel *The Da Vinci Code* the author, Dan Brown, speaks of the "divine feminine" as the hope of humanity. In this view of things, "patriarchy" [responsible male leadership, reflecting God's creation of order and distinction] is the demonic center of an odious power-obsessed hierarchy that places the male over the female, mind over body, heaven over earth, the transcendent creator God over the created world. It must be replaced with a profoundly pagan, feministic, pantheistic sense of divinity as the life-force within all things, a world of the yin and the yang where nothing is ultimately right or wrong.

These two mutually-exclusive, all-inclusive programs of the pagan and the biblical worldview are presently locked in deadly confrontation. In this clash, gender, whether exclusive heterosexuality or liberated pan-sexuality, has a leading, integral, and logical part in the whole web of ideas.

This is not a moment to retreat in fear, but an occasion for full-orbed biblical witness. This radically divided issue of gender allows us to:

—seize the occasion of religious clarity that the face-off of these two worldviews allows;

—thoroughly understand the system of paganism better than the average person so as to engage our contemporaries in serious worldview exchange;

—make the issues clear for our rising generations of young believers so that when they go off to college they will have the courage to speak in spite of the intimidating, mind-numbing, politically-correct speech of the average campus;

—reach those who are disillusioned with the empty promises of pagan egalitarianism and bring to them the liberating truth of biblical, divinely inspired wisdom.

Christians, and in particular, Christian women, must understand these issues. This is a unique moment for faithful women to know their Bibles, understand the biblical worldview, and make sure their voices are heard. This is why it is absolutely essential that the church equip women to speak to the burning issues of the culture by being trained in the disciplines of theology and apologetics. This is why it is essential, according to the biblical pattern, that Christian women disciple other women to know and live the truths of biblical womanhood in the church and in the world.

Biblical Foundations for Womanhood resources that amplify concepts in this chapter:

• A covenantal approach to discipleship/Christian education: *Heirs of the Covenant.*

• Titus 2:3-5: *Spiritual Mothering; The Legacy of Biblical Womanhood,* Chapters 4 and 12.

NOTES:

1. John Calvin, *Institutes of the Christian Religion,* ed. John T. McNeill, translated and indexed by Ford Lewis Battles (Philadelphia: The Westminster Press), 1011-1012.

2. John Stott, *Guard the Truth* (Downers Grove, IL: InterVarsity Press, 1996), 185-186.

3. *Westminster Larger Catechism* (Atlanta: Committee for Christian Education & Publications, 1990).

4 Charles H. Dunahoo, *Making Kingdom Disciples* (Phillipsburg, NJ: P & R Publishing, 2005), 11-12.

5. George Grant, lecture at Franklin Classical Christian School, Franklin, TN.

6. Stott, *Guard the Truth,* 188.

7. W. E. Vine, *An Expository Dictionary of New Testament Words,* Vol. IV (Old Tappan, NJ: Fleming H. Revell, 1940), 44.

8. R. Kent Hughes and Bryan Chapell, *1 & 2 Timothy and Titus: To Guard The Deposit* (Wheaton, IL: Crossway Books, 2000), 328-329.

9

2 Timothy 3:1-17 — Scripture

God begets and multiplies his Church only by means of his word. It is by the preaching of the grace of God alone that the Church is kept from perishing.

JOHN CALVIN[1]

Ligon's fifth reason that a church should have a women's ministry is:

The denial or the twisting of the Bible's clear teaching on manhood and womanhood is one of the central ways that biblical authority is being undermined in our times. That's why Bruce Ware has said, "To the extent that [giving in on these issues of gender and sexuality] occurs, the church establishes a pattern of following cultural pressures and urgings against the clear authority of God's written word. When this happens . . . the church becomes desensitized to Scripture's radical call and forms, instead, a taste for worldly accolades. . . . To compromise on a little thing will pave the way for compromises on much that matters."

The church has been called to shape culture, not ape it. But very often our churches reflect rather than constructively influence worldly culture. Even worse, some church leaders tell us that if we want to reach the culture, we must become like the culture. Don't you love the way

Dorothy Sayers confronted this mixed-up notion? She said: "It is not the business of the church to conform Christ to men, but men to Christ." That's precisely the challenge we face in the area of biblical manhood and womanhood. Will the church conform her values to the prevailing cultural mores and norms, or will we impact and influence and shape our culture?

Of course, behind and underneath this is the fundamental issue of biblical authority. If you can write off, ignore, or distort the Bible's teaching in this area, as crystal-clear as it is, then you can do so with anything the Bible teaches. Indeed, the Bible is so clear and blunt on this that sometimes it is hard for ministers to stand in the pulpit and read aloud certain biblical passages, knowing the kind of reaction they may provoke in hearers who have been steeped in a feminist culture alien to the biblical-complementarian thought-world of the Scriptures. But if you can change what the Bible says on this, you can make the Bible say whatever you want it to say. Thus, the manhood-womanhood issue becomes a scriptural authority issue. Is our pattern in the church going to be to do a hermeneutical twist whenever we come to an issue where the Bible's teaching makes us culturally uncomfortable, or are we going to let the lion loose, let God be God, and let His Word speak and rule in our lives? So, fundamentally this is a scriptural authority issue. Just think how women's ministry has the capacity of dealing with that in a unique way.

The text for this chapter shows that Scripture is the unequivocal keystone of a women's ministry in the church.

THE TEXT — 2 TIMOTHY 3:6-7, 14-15

For among them are those who creep into households and capture weak women, burdened with sins and led astray by various passions, always learning and never able to arrive at a knowledge of the truth. . . . But as for you, continue in what you have learned and have firmly believed, knowing from whom you learned it and how from childhood you have been acquainted with the sacred writings, which are able to make you wise for salvation through faith in Christ Jesus.

Paul was in prison when he wrote 2 Timothy; he knew death was imminent. This is his final letter. It is incredibly personal and poignant, but it is not private. It is for the church throughout the ages.

In this chapter Paul summons Timothy, and us, to continue. He contrasts those who continue in the gospel and those who do not. Then, in dramatic and climactic fashion, he points to the Scriptures, the authority and anchor for continuing.

Once again I am breathless at the apologetic for a women's ministry that develops throughout these letters. In this text we are confronted with the undeniable need and the unequivocal keystone for a women's ministry in the local church.

The Undeniable Need for a Women's Ministry

Paul begins by profiling the lovers of self in the "last days," or the time between the first and second comings of Christ. So this characterization is typical of all ages.

> But understand this, that in the last days there will come times of difficulty. For people will be lovers of self, lovers of money, proud, arrogant, abusive, disobedient to their parents, ungrateful, unholy, heartless, unappeasable, slanderous, without self-control, brutal, not loving good, treacherous, reckless, swollen with conceit, lovers of pleasure rather than lovers of God, having the appearance of godliness, but denying its power. (vv. 1-5)

This chilling description of "lovers of self" is unsettling because it describes garden-variety selfishness that we all battle. It is disconcerting because these people appear godly. But how often are we arrogant, heartless, and slanderous on the way to church and then enter the church with an appearance of godliness? The problem is that between the car and the church there is no repentance, and thus no transforming gospel power. Paul warns us to "avoid such people," and then he exposes their strategy, which, interestingly, is the same as Satan's in the Garden—they sneak in and invert the creation order by going to the women. The households they crept into were probably the homes where the house churches met; so these are women in the church.

This is not a blanket indictment of all women. Paul carefully explains that women who are vulnerable to false teachers are "weak women, burdened with sins and led astray by various passions" (v. 6).

> Those whom the false teachers seek to capture are designated with . . . a diminutive . . . literally "little women," which is used here with a negative connotation. It is the immaturity and thus the weakness of these "childish women" that make them susceptible to the false teachers. Paul does not use the term to derogate women but to describe a situation involving particular women. That he uses a diminutive form shows that he is not intending to describe women in general.
>
> The reason that these women are characterized as childish and weak is given in two qualifying participial clauses. The passive participle . . . means here "overwhelmed," and its perfect tense specifies that this is a condition that these women are continually in. . . . They are overwhelmed by their "sins." . . .
>
> Not only are they overwhelmed by past sins, they are being continually led in the present . . . by a multitude of desires . . . specifically of evil desires. . . . That their consciences are burdened by past sins and their lives controlled by such desires puts them in a weakened condition and makes them vulnerable to false teachers who "capture" them as followers.[2]

One wonders about the sins that burdened these women and led them astray. It seems obvious that they were not functioning under ecclesiastical authority. It is unlikely that they were spending their time in ministries of covenantal compassion. Their doctrine of community was faulty because they were willing to follow divisive teachers. They apparently were not involved in discipleship relationships with godly women who would guide them to maturity. Their lives were already inconsistent with the principles of biblical womanhood; so their propensity was to follow the false rather than the true. These women were lovers of self and not lovers of God; so they were life-takers and not life-givers.

Once immature women are captured by unsound doctrine, they begin a never-ending, self-indulgent quest for knowledge. They are "always learning and never able to arrive at a knowledge of the truth" (v. 7). Paul has already equated a knowledge of the truth with salvation (1 Timothy 2:3-4).

This profile establishes the undeniable need for mature women to invest in the lives of immature women with the prayer that "God may perhaps grant them repentance leading to a knowledge of the truth, and they may escape from the snare of the devil, after being captured by him to do his will" (2 Timothy 2:25-26). Then Paul supplies an example of female maturity and shows the source of this maturity.

The Unequivocal Keystone of a Women's Ministry

As Paul charges Timothy to be a lover of God who continues in the gospel, he reminds him of the women in Timothy's life.

> But as for you, continue in what you have learned and have firmly believed, knowing from whom you learned it and how from childhood you have been acquainted with the sacred writings. (vv. 14-15)

This is the second time he has used the memory of these women to encourage Timothy to persevere. In Chapter 1 he wrote:

> I am reminded of your sincere faith, a faith that dwelt first in your grand-mother Lois and your mother Eunice and now, I am sure, dwells in you as well. For this reason I remind you to fan into flame the gift of God. (vv. 5-6)

Eunice was married to an unbeliever. We can only imagine the prayer, grace, wisdom, and strength required for these two women to teach Timothy the Scriptures. They also kept Timothy involved in church life. The believers knew him well.

> Paul came also to Derbe and to Lystra. A disciple was there, named Timothy, the son of a Jewish woman who was a believer, but his father was a Greek. He was well spoken of by the brothers at Lystra and Iconium. Paul wanted Timothy to accompany him, and he took him and circumcised him because of the Jews who were in those places, for they all knew that his father was a Greek. (Acts 16:1-3)

There is no mention that Eunice's husband objected to his wife and mother-in-law teaching Timothy the Scriptures and taking him to church or to Timothy's missionary calling. This lack of resistance is remarkable.

Surely the rest of the story is one of Eunice's obedience to the scriptural admonition to wives of unbelieving husbands: "Likewise, wives, be subject to your own husbands, so that even if some do not obey the word, they may be won without a word by the conduct of their wives—when they see your respectful and pure conduct" (1 Peter 3:1-2). Perhaps it was this less-than-perfect situation that shaped and matured Eunice. She had to know and obey God's Word in hard places.

Another fascinating side of the story is Lois's relationship with her daughter and her son-in-law. Was she the one who taught Eunice to love and respect her husband? Did she help Eunice navigate those difficult issues of teaching Timothy to honor and respect his father while teaching him to love God's Word and God's way? Was she the Titus 2 woman in Eunice's life?

Reminding Timothy of these two women would bring to his mind a kaleidoscope of memories of Scripture applied to daily relationships and circumstances. This set the stage for one of the most comprehensive statements of the power of Holy Scripture to transform us from lovers of self to lovers of God.

> . . . *from childhood you have been acquainted with the sacred writings, which are able to make you wise for salvation through faith in Christ Jesus. All Scripture is breathed out by God and profitable for teaching, for reproof, for correction, and for training in righteousness, that the man of God may be competent, equipped for every good work. (vv. 15-17)*

"When the Spirit of truth . . . guides [us] into all the truth" (John 16:13), redeemed women are made wise, competent, and equipped for the good work of womanhood. God's Word is the undeniable keystone for life and ministry.

> *And when Moses had finished speaking all these words to all Israel, he said to them, "Take to heart all the words by which I am warning you today. . . . For it is no empty word for you, but your very life."* (Deuteronomy 32:45-47)

> *For as the rain and the snow come down from heaven and do not return there but water the earth, making it bring forth and sprout, giving seed*

to the sower and bread to the eater, so shall my word be that goes out from my mouth; it shall not return to me empty, but it shall accomplish that which I purpose, and shall succeed in the thing for which I sent it. (Isaiah 55:10-11)

For the word of God is living and active, sharper than any two-edged sword, piercing to the division of soul and of spirit, of joints and of marrow, and discerning the thoughts and intentions of the heart. (Hebrews 4:12)

BIBLICAL EXAMPLE

The women in 2 Timothy 3 are the examples. The childish women crumbled. But Lois and Eunice were rooted in God's Word and stood firm. The Old Testament gives a graphic description of this contrast:

But Lot's wife, behind him, looked back, and she became a pillar of salt. (Genesis 19:26)

. . . our daughters [will be] like corner pillars cut for the structure of a palace. (Psalm 144:12b)

Two different Hebrew words are translated "pillar" in these verses. The two words illustrate two kinds of women in the church. Some are pillars of salt, and some are pillars of stone.

God sent angels to warn Lot that He was going to destroy the city. The angels urged, "Escape for your life. Do not look back or stop anywhere in the valley. Escape to the hills, lest you be swept away" (Genesis 19:17). Lot's wife looked back, and she became a pillar of salt. The Hebrew word translated "pillar" in this verse is *nesib*. "The obvious intent here is to depict her as stopped, trapped, transformed as and where she was, in a still upright posture."[3]

Lot's wife epitomizes weak women who are easily led astray by their self-indulgent passions. The root issue is authority. They do not obey God's Word, so they are controlled by personal happiness rather than by God's glory. They are concerned about the present rather than the eternal. They are trapped in static immaturity. They may dazzle us with their seemingly picture-perfect lives and their brilliant self-sufficiency, but simmering just under the surface is insecurity, jealousy, and superficiality. It is a pseudo-strength that easily disintegrates. Sadly, they often think they have all the answers. They don't realize they are at risk. Two marks of maturity are submission to God's Word and a teachable heart that listens to and learns from others.

In Psalm 144, David calls on the Lord to "Rescue me and deliver me from the hand of foreigners" (v. 11). Then, in the last few verses, he pictures the blessings that come with deliverance from our enemies. One of those blessings is that the next generation will flourish. He envisions daughters as corner pillars who have been cut for a palace. The word translated "pillar" refers not to a free-standing pillar, but to a corner, supporting pillar. The word translated "cut" is "used especially of hewn stones."[4] The word translated "palace" refers to a palace or temple. So David was thinking of women who have been shaped and smoothed to serve God's purpose in the home and church.

> The paraphrase of Bishop Patrick, doubtless, conveys the real meaning: "Tall and beautiful, like those polished pillars which are the ornaments of a palace." . . . It is remarkable that the Greeks made use of pilasters, called Caryatides, (carved after the figure of a woman dressed in long robes,) to support the entablatures of their buildings.[5]

These corner pillars were both beautiful and functional. They gave grace and dignity to the structure even as they supported it. If these pillars weakened, the structure was in danger. David considers these women to be gifts from God. He brings the Psalm to a rousing conclusion: "Blessed are the people to whom such blessings fall! Blessed are the people whose God is the LORD!" "LORD," or Yahweh, is God's personal name conveying covenant faithfulness to His people. He is "LORD" to those He has sovereignly claimed as His own. He lives in intimate relationship with them. His Word is their authority, His glory is their purpose, He is their sufficiency, and He is their strength.*

Unless corner pillars stand on a firm foundation, they will topple. Lois and Eunice were corner pillars. Their God was the Lord. They were thoroughly equipped by God's Word to stand strong and to give the legacy of truth to the next generation. They are exemplars of the disciples Jesus described when He said, "If you abide in my word, you are truly my disciples, and you will know the truth, and the truth will set you free" (John 8:31-32).

The Task

The Bible should be the centerpiece of a women's ministry. It should form the infrastructure of everything the women's ministry does, but often churches take a pragmatic approach to women's Bible studies. Some are personality-driven studies where women gather around a gifted teacher. Some are even nonpersonal with teaching via technology. Some are needs-based studies where women decide to study a specific topic of common interest. These studies are usually autonomous. They are disconnected from the pulpit ministry and from other components of the women's ministry. They often, perhaps unintentionally, duplicate or compete rather than coordinate with other discipleship ministries in the church. The problem may not be what takes place in the Bible studies; it is what does not take place. A random approach always has systemic weaknesses. There needs to be a principled and personal approach that gives theological, educational, and relational integrity to women's Bible studies. We will consider two of the tasks of the leadership of a women's ministry.

The Bible is to have a controlling influence in our lives and in our ministry in the local church. . . . The people and the house we serve are not ours; they are His. It is vital that we live and minister in accordance with His Book. This is completely counterintuitive in our pragmatic culture. We want to minister our way. We want to set up *our* own rules and define the game plan. But Paul emphasizes that if we are to grow in grace as a congregation, if we are to be what He has called us to be, we have to live and minister according to the Book. (Ligon Duncan)

First, the leadership should formulate an overarching purpose for women's Bible studies that assimilates the principles we have seen in the Pastoral Letters.

• *Ecclesiastical submission:* Bible study teachers and materials should be under the oversight of the elders, and these teachers should lead the women to support the male leadership of the church. This is not only true for women. This should be the policy for all educational ministries.

• *Covenantal compassion:* The Bible studies should teach women the theological reasons for ministries of compassion and provide opportunities for women to show compassion.

• *Covenantal community:* Bible studies should be a time when women learn the theology of community, are enfolded into relationships with other women, and are mobilized to be supporting pillars in the church. Bible studies should teach women to see immature women, even rebellious ones, not with disdain but with a desire to mother them to maturity.

• *Discipleship:* Bible studies should equip women to pass on the legacy of biblical womanhood to the next generation and should offer opportunities for them to have hands-on experiences in discipling one another.

Second, the leadership should determine how and when women are discipled in first principles of biblical womanhood.

A friend moved to a new city. Her family settled into a church where God's Word was faithfully preached, and she began attending a women's Bible study. But after several weeks she e-mailed me that she had a growing concern. "The church is great and the women's ministry is active, but the more I get to know the women the more I realize that they think like feminists. There is a disconnect between their belief in Scripture and their application of Scripture to their lives as women. How can this be?"

I asked her where women were learning basic principles of biblical womanhood. Several weeks later she responded, "I've looked and listened and I cannot find anyplace where these women are confronted with these truths."

Unfortunately this is a common problem.

Churches are filled with women who have traded their birthright as corner pillars to engage in a prideful pursuit of knowledge. They have stopped short of true discipleship that moves from knowledge to wisdom— the application of truth into life.* They have perfected some Bible study skills, but they do not know how to live as godly, chaste single women, or love their husbands, or care for the sick and oppressed, or support the male leadership of the church. They are often critical of the men in the church. They have selfish hearts rather than servant hearts. They have not been taught all that Jesus commanded in His Word about their design and calling. They need to grow up. They desperately need an apprenticeship with mature Christian women who will train them in the craft of womanhood.

The crisis of womanhood is so critical that there is no time for a culture of inertia in the church. Feminism is the only paradigm for womanhood that many women and girls have ever considered. It takes a radical paradigm shift to understand the essentials of biblical womanhood. It takes grace-animated obedience to God's Word to live biblical womanhood. Women's Bible studies are the apparatus the church can utilize to educate and equip women to stand tall and brave in the war for womanhood.

In one of his novels, the nineteenth-century author George MacDonald described a beloved village teacher. "He would never contradict anything but would oppose error only by teaching truth. He presented truth and set it face to face with error in the minds of his students, leaving the two sides and the growing intellect, heart, and conscience to fight that matter out. To him the business of the teacher was to rouse and urge this battle by leading fresh forces of truth onto the field."[6]

Teachers of women's Bible studies should be equipped to lead fresh forces of the truth of womanhood onto the field with confidence that God's Word does not return to Him empty.

Above all, leaders of women should pray for the women they lead. Pray that they will exclaim with the psalmist, "Oh how I love your law! It is my meditation all the day. . . . How sweet are your words to my taste, sweeter than honey to my mouth. . . . Your word is a lamp to my feet and a light to my path. . . . Your testimonies are my heritage forever, for they are the joy of my heart" (Psalm 119:97, 103, 105, 111).

THE TOOLS

Some resources to equip Bible teachers for this kind of covenantal, complementarian, integrative ministry are:

• The pastor and elders

Meetings with the pastor, other staff people, and elders can keep Bible teachers connected to the doctrine and direction of the church so they can teach the women to love and support the church. There may be times when Bible studies can coordinate with the sermons, or with a church-wide Christian education emphasis.

• The women's ministry leadership

There should be a system for the women's ministry leadership to give oversight and communicate with the Bible teachers. Then the teachers can support programs and activities by teaching the biblical reason for these ministries.

• *Biblical Foundations for Womanhood* (see page 27 for a list of these materials)

The topical studies can equip teachers to weave foundational principles of biblical womanhood into whatever they are teaching. The Bible studies provide a model that incorporates the principles of this book into lesson plans.

• A team

It is difficult for a Bible study teacher to plan community-building activities and ministries of compassion in addition to preparing lessons. A covenantal approach means that the Bible study teacher does not function in isolation. The women's leadership can appoint a group of women to work alongside the teacher to plan all of the aspects of the Bible study except the lesson. For example, this committee could:

Prepare refreshments.

Have greeters so women are warmly welcomed.

Arrange for discussion leaders and/or small group prayer leaders.

Plan short testimonies so women get to know each other's stories of God's grace.

Have women sign cards for missionaries.

Periodically, in place of the Bible study lesson, plan a ministry opportunity such as visiting homebound members or volunteering at a homeless shelter.

Plan occasional fellowship times such as a meal in someone's home.

See Appendix 3 for examples of guidelines to help evaluate Bible study materials.

In summary, the following questions can help a leadership team to be intentional in adhering to the principles discussed in this book. Use these questions to plan and implement every study, event, project, and activity. Every activity or ministry will not accomplish all of these, but each activity should accomplish some of them.

- Why are we doing this?
- How will this glorify God by reflecting His character?
- How will the gospel be presented?
- How will this teach women to think biblically?
- What will this teach women about biblical womanhood?
- What will this teach women about living covenantally?
- How will this build community among the women?
- How will it build community with other members, age groups, and ministries of the church?
- How will this extend the boundaries of the community to enfold those outside the church?
- How will this demonstrate the compassion of Jesus?
- What characteristic of the covenant does this express?
- Will what we do and how we do it have a life-giving or a life-taking effect in our church?
- Will what we do and how we do it help or hinder the leaders of our church?
- How will we communicate our answers to the above questions to the church so they understand why we do what we do?

Pastor Chuck Betters, Glasgow Reformed Presbyterian Church, Bear, Delaware, coauthor with Sharon Betters of TREASURES OF FAITH

As a seasoned pastor who experienced severe church conflict in a previous church, I understand the critical need for men and women to view all of life through the grid of God's Word. The peace and prosperity of the local church depends on all of its members understanding how to apply sound doctrine to daily life as well as to Body life. Our church views church life as a marble cake. This means that all ministries intentionally look for ways to partner with other ministries in order to build God's Kingdom within the context of the vision of our church. The women's ministry leadership team has caught this vision. They sometimes choose Bible study topics that reinforce the message of the sermons. When I preached a series titled "David, a Man After God's Own Heart," they chose as their theme for the year "A Woman After God's Own Heart." When I preached a series titled "Becoming a Redemptive Presence," they chose topics that helped women practically apply that message.

A few years after I started shepherding this baby church, I was thankful to see that every woman in church leadership had come through the women's ministry. It was in women's Bible studies that they learned how to live out their roles as women in the church and were confronted with the command that women are to use all of their gifts to build God's Kingdom. It was in the women's ministry that they learned how to study Scripture and what it means to be a helper in the church.

When a woman needs an older woman to befriend or mentor her, I have great confidence asking a woman who has been trained through our Bible study ministry to come alongside her. Our elders agree that without these scripturally grounded women, our task would be much more difficult. Our observation is that when women understand their role as helpers and partners in ministry, they resolve conflicts that probably would end up at the feet of the elders in many churches.

Biblical Foundations for Womanhood resources that amplify concepts in this chapter:

• A covenantal perspective of Scripture: *Heirs of the Covenant*, Chapter 3.

• The teaching process: *Heirs of the Covenant*, Chapter 6.

• Psalm 144:12b: *The Legacy of Biblical Womanhood*, Chapter 3.

NOTES:

1. John Calvin, *Calvin's Wisdom, An Anthology Arranged Alphabetically*, ed. Graham Miller (Carlisle, PA: The Banner of Truth Trust, 1992), 60.

2. George Knight, III, *The Pastoral Epistles*, The New International Greek Testament Commentary (Grand Rapids, MI: Eerdmans, 1992), 433-434.

3. R. Laird Harris, Gleason L. Archer, Jr., Bruce K. Waltke, *Theological Wordbook of the Old Testament*, Vol. 2 (Chicago: Moody Press, 1980), 592.

4. Ibid., 157.

5. Footnote in *Calvin's Commentaries*, Vol. VI, trans. Rev. James Anderson (Grand Rapids, MI: Baker Book House, 1981), 267.

6. George MacDonald, *The Fisherman's Lady*, ed. Michael R. Phillips (Minneapolis: Bethany House, 1982), 39.

10

Conclusion

We are God's people, the chosen of the Lord,
Born of His Spirit, established by His Word;
Our cornerstone is Christ alone, and strong in Him we stand:
O let us live transparently, and walk heart to heart and hand in hand.
We are the Body of which the Lord is Head,
Called to obey Him, now risen from the dead;
He wills us be a family, diverse yet truly one:
O let us give our gifts to God, and so shall His work on earth be done.

BRYAN JEFFERY LEECH[1]

FROM LIGON

In Chapters Four through Nine Susan unfolded a biblical apologetic for women's ministry in the church. In each chapter, at the conclusion of the Task section, she called leaders of women to pray for the women they lead. The priority of prayer cannot be overstated. I can think of no more fitting way to conclude this book than to encourage women who serve Christ in His church to be women who pray for His church.

Paul's letters are filled with prayer. The prayer recorded in Ephesians 3:14-19 shows us what God wants His church to look like.

> *For this reason, I bow my knees before the Father, from whom every fam-*
> *ily in heaven and on earth is named, that according to the riches of his*
> *glory he may grant you to be strengthened with power through his Spirit*

in your inner being, so that Christ may dwell in your hearts through faith—that you, being rooted and grounded in love, may have strength to comprehend with all the saints what is the breadth and length and height and depth, and to know the love of Christ that surpasses knowledge, that you may be filled with all the fullness of God.

Before considering the petitions, notice the approach and shape of this prayer.

The way Paul approaches the Lord in prayer is so instructive. He prays to the Father. He's conscious that through Jesus Christ he now has a heavenly Father. Notice his reverent approach to the Father—he bows his knees. Our heavenly Father is the Creator of the universe, the just Judge, the One who is the Lord of hosts who is as terrible as an army with banners. He pierces the heart, He discerns the motives and the conscience, and when we come before Him we are to come with reverence and awe. The language "I bow my knees" is not the polite language of kneeling at an Anglican prayer bench. This is prostration before the Lord of Glory. Paul then acknowledges that his Father is the only One he can come to; there are no alternatives. He is the Father of every family in heaven and on earth; He is the one true God.

The Trinitarian shape of this prayer is also instructive. Paul prays *to the Father*, that they would be strengthened *through the Spirit*, in order that *Christ* would dwell in their hearts. The doctrine of the Trinity is not a theoretical abstraction to be left to the professionals to consider. It is essential to who God is and how He works in our lives. All New Testament prayers revel in various aspects of the glory of who God is. When a husband relates to his wife the way he should, he revels in who she is. Can you imagine a husband saying, "I'll leave it to someone else to figure out who you are and I'll take care of practical matters"? God wants us to revel in who He is in prayer.

Paul's petitions for the Ephesian Christians gives a beautiful outline of the kinds of intercessions we should make for one another so that we will look like the bride of Christ. I cannot think of a better list of petitions for women to pray for their family, friends, fellow congregation members, sisters in Christ, pastors and their wives, and elders and their wives. There are at least five petitions.

. . . that according to the riches of his glory he may grant you to be strengthened with power through his Spirit in your inner being . . .

The first thing that Paul prays for is that the Ephesian Christians will be given spiritual strength for the work, life, ministry, and duty to which they were called. In this petition Paul prays that we as God's people will be strengthened in the inner man by a power that does not come from within ourselves. He prays that we will be given spiritual strength according to the riches of God's glory. There is no limit to God's glory, so there is more than enough to supply the strength we need in our inmost being. Paul prays that we will be strengthened from the inside out with a power that does not come from within. This is a radically different thought from the major views that exist in our culture and in the world. Paganism is on the march. Postmodernism often simply carries along with it forms of paganism, and one of the most popular beliefs is to "look within" and discover the hidden strength within you. Motivational speakers, including pastors, tell us to discover the giant, or the champion, within. Frankly, I do not want to discover the giant within me.

Christianity says that when we discover what is in us, we have only begun the quest for salvation, because when we discover what is in us, we have just found out what is wrong in this world. We must look outside ourselves to find a Champion. Paul does not tell us to find something within us to give us what we need to live the Christian life. He knows that we need to be strengthened in the very depths of our souls, but we need that strength from somewhere other than our own souls. It is the Holy Spirit who strengthens us with His power in the inner man.

The bride of Christ knows that she is called to do things she does not have the strength to do, and she knows that the Holy Spirit supplies that strength. So if we are going to look like the bride of Christ, we must live in dependence upon the spiritual strength that only God can supply. One way this will manifest itself is prayer. Prayer itself is an act of continual confession that we do not have what we need in ourselves to live and minister as we are called to do and that we look to our heavenly Father to supply our need.

Margaret was a nurse. While working at the hospital one day, those who were at home looking after the children lost track of her two-year-old child for just a few minutes. They began frantically searching the house and discovered him, unconscious, in the swimming pool. They attempted to resuscitate the child, he was airlifted to a pediatric trauma unit, and there they waited thirty-six hours while the doctors did everything they could. Finally the doctors said life was slipping away from this child. The family gathered in the room. Doctors who had watched this family trust the Lord through this horrific trauma gathered with them. Margaret turned to me as she held her child and said, "Could we sing the Doxology?" As the child slipped out of this world into the world to come, those in that room sang, "Praise God from whom all blessings flow; praise Him, all creatures here below; praise Him above, ye heav'nly host; praise Father, Son, and Holy Ghost."

What gave Margaret the strength to sing praise to the One who had given and the One who had taken away? She had been strengthened within by a power that was not her own.

You may not be called to do things that are dramatic. Your calling may be to love a recalcitrant, uncooperative husband. Or it may be to minister to young children and tell them the word of truth day after day. Or it may be a ministry in the church that takes you out of your comfort zone. But the truth is, all of the Christian life, and all ministry, is beyond the limits of our own personal power and abilities. Ministry begins at the end of our own competencies and abilities.

What a wonderful petition to pray for one another: "Lord, strengthen her within to deal with the infidelity of her husband." "Lord, strengthen her within to continue to bear up with that older child, who unlike her other children has strayed far from You." "Lord, strengthen her within to teach her sisters in Christ about the truths of Scripture." "Lord, strengthen her within to continue to minister to her family day by day even as she cares for an older parent in her home who is disrupting family life." "Lord, strengthen her through Your Spirit to be and do what You have called her to be and do."

> *. . . so that Christ may dwell in your hearts through faith . . .*

The second petition shows that the purpose of the Spirit's work in our inner being is that Christ might dwell in us. Notice the order. The work of the Spirit is so that we get Christ. The Holy Spirit always points to Christ; He enables us to receive Christ, to trust Christ, to have faith in Christ. Also notice the way that Christ dwells in our hearts—by faith. How do we get Christ? By faith. How do we experience the forgiveness, mercy, grace, and power of Christ? By faith. Faith alone—not faith plus something else—is the means whereby we receive all the benefits of Christ. And this faith does not originate within us; the Source is the Triune God.

To be indwelt by Christ means that our hearts, the very essence of our minds, wills, and affections, the core of our inner being, becomes a suitable habitation for Christ. Suppose you move into a new home that is a fixer-upper. Gradually you replace the horrendous wallpaper, the garish colors, and the outmoded fixtures until, over time, your friends comment that your home reflects your personality and tastes. It suits your family. They know it is your home because it looks like a place you would have made. In this phrase Paul tells us that the Holy Spirit does a work of interior decoration in us so that we become a suitable habitation for the Lord Jesus Christ. People begin to recognize that our desires and priorities look like Christ.

> . . . that you, being rooted and grounded in love . . .

In the third petition Paul prays that our apprehension of God's love will compel us to love Him and love our neighbor. To use John's language, "We love because he first loved us" (1 John 4:19). When we are rooted and grounded in God's love for us, the affections and desires of our soul will be fixed on Him, and that will result in a love to Him and a love to our neighbor.

> . . . that you . . . may have strength to comprehend with all the saints what is the breadth and length and height and depth, and to know the love of Christ that surpasses knowledge . . .

In the fourth petition Paul prays that we will be awash with an experiential knowledge of the love of God in Christ for us. The language is magnificent. He wants us to know the limitless love of Christ that surpasses knowledge. Apparently, there were people in Ephesus who were peddling "secret knowledge" as the key to the Christian life. In the second century this grew into a full-blown religious movement that became known as Gnosticism. The Gnostics taught that the key to the Christian life is knowing secrets that were passed on from super-spiritual Christians who had secret knowledge. It seems that Paul undermined that notion by saying, "I am praying that *all* the Ephesian Christians will know the love of Christ that surpasses knowledge."

I am a Presbyterian, and a Presbyterian preoccupation is that we want to understand and write a discourse on everything. We want to understand the peace that passes understanding. But some things go beyond the capacity of human understanding—this is why we must pray for it. Paul prays that we will know this love that surpasses knowledge because it is necessary for our spiritual maturity. We will not be rooted and grounded in the Christian life until we know this love that surpasses knowledge.

In his wonderful book *A Call to Spiritual Reformation*, Don Carson, commenting on this passage, tells the story of a colleague at Trinity Evangelical Divinity School. The man and his wife were foster parents. They kept babies until they were placed into permanent adoptive homes. Social services contacted this couple and asked if they would consider taking eighteen-month-old twin boys. The couple agreed and later found out that the boys had been passed from home to home (eight to be exact), and in some of those homes they had been physically abused. Psychologists said that the abuse had been so severe that the children would never be normal affectively. The first night the boys were in this home, the couple put them to bed and then after a while went to their room to check on them, only to find them silently sobbing, their pillows wet with tears. They did not want to be heard because in their experience, when they cried they were beaten. The boys were in this home longer than expected (not the six weeks the agency had promised, but something like two years), yet finally they were placed in a loving, adoptive home. When they were psychologically retested for their adoptive placement, amazingly, the boys were judged to be normal affectively. They responded emotionally like any healthy child responds to parents and to other nurturing figures in their life. What had happened? They had experienced the love of parents the way God intends children to experience the love of parents. Parental love had matured and healed them.

If you have not experienced the love of your heavenly Father, you will not be able to grow up to maturity. I have known godly women who wrestled with knowing whether their heavenly Father loves them, and often this is tied to their own experience of deficit in their relationship with their earthly father or with significant men in their lives. But this deficit can be reversed just as it was with those twin boys. If this is your experience, pray that God will give you strength to comprehend His love that surpasses knowledge. If your sister in Christ struggles with this, stand in the gap for her just as that couple did for those little boys. Pray that God will minister His love through His people to those who have experienced deficits in their own lives and that God will give them the capacity to know His love that surpasses knowledge.

. . . that you may be filled with all the fullness of God . . .

At first-read this final petition seems simple, but in fact it is measureless in meaning. I do not know all that Paul is asking for in this petition, but I think he means at least this: in Scripture the term "the fullness of God" is often a picture of the fullness of what He is. So this is a prayer that we would be the fullness of His image. Paul has been stacking up petitions to lead to this grand climax—that we will be all that God intends us to be, that we will look like our heavenly Father.

When people visit our home, they usually notice two pictures on a table in the living room. One is a picture of my dad at nineteen or twenty years old in a Marine Corps uniform. The other is a picture of me as a sophomore in college, in a typical college blue blazer. Most people say, "I didn't know you were in the military," and I respond, "I wasn't. That's my dad." Almost invariably they remark, "You look exactly like your dad." I love it when people say that because I am not half the man that my father was. I love my dad, and I love it when people tell me that I look like him. In this passage Paul says, "I pray that when people see you they will say, 'She looks so much like her heavenly Father. I see what her Father is like in what she loves, in the way she lives, in the way she ministers, in her desires and priorities. She looks like her heavenly Father.'"

What does the bride of the Lord Jesus Christ look like? Her heavenly Father.

The church needs women who will embark on the grand and glorious adventure of knowing and serving God, and along the way they will probably be unaware that they look more and more like their Father.

A final word to my fellow pastors and elders: Women who embark on this journey need your prayers. I ask you to join me in praying that these sisters in Christ will be strengthened with power by the Holy Spirit in their inmost being so that Christ might dwell in their hearts by faith, that they would be rooted and grounded in love, that they will know the love of Christ that surpasses knowledge, and that they will be filled up to all the fullness of God.

FROM SUSAN

Writing a book is sweet fellowship with the Lord. He instructs me as I write. If no one ever reads it, His purpose has been accomplished in my own soul. I am satisfied. If He is pleased to use it in the lives of others, may He be glorified.

My heart rejoiced as the Holy Spirit opened my eyes to the apologetic for women's ministry in the Pastoral Letters. My convictions were strengthened as I realized that the strength of this apologetic is not in the parts but in the whole. The interdependence of submission, compassion, community, discipleship, and Scripture reflects the unity of the Trinity. This covenantal unity is a distinguishing feature of a biblical world-and-life view. It is redemptive thinking and living. Writing this book recharged my passion for women in God's church to be life-giving helpers who nurture this unity, but throughout the writing process a question hovered over my mind: Does Paul tell us what kind of woman it takes to lead other women to fulfill this calling?

I was not disappointed. I found the answer in the last words of Paul's last letter.

Greet Prisca and Aquila, and the household of Onesiphorus. Erastus remained at Corinth, and I left Trophimus, who was ill, at Miletus. Do your best to come before winter. Eubulus sends greetings to you, as do

Pudens and Linus and Claudia and all the brothers. The Lord be with your
spirit. Grace be with you. (2 Timothy 4:19-22)

At first I struggled with these final words from Paul's pen. Is a list of
people and places the most significant thing he had to say? Ah, my question reveals the problem. I am stuck at the knowledge level. It is one
thing to think biblically, but the rub comes when I am confronted with
living covenantally.

In a dungeon awaiting death, Paul's theology pushed him to the transcendent wonder of covenant life. His dying desire was for the Lord to
be with his family. The word translated "brothers" (*adelphoi*) "refers to
siblings in a family. In New Testament usage, depending on the context,
adelphoi may refer either to men or to both men and women who are siblings (brothers and sisters) in God's family, the church."[2]

My mind cannot comprehend the grandeur of gospel unity, but I
long to grow in this grace because I am convinced that a theology of
home and family is essential for a discipler of women. I am not mini-
mizing skills and experience,* but first and foremost Christianity is
about a Person and a place that determines our perspective of people and
places. One of the people Paul mentions is Prisca, or Priscilla. She is my
case in point. Consider what we know about her.

Paul left Athens and went to Corinth. And he found a Jew named Aquila,
a native of Pontus, recently come from Italy with his wife Priscilla, because
Claudius had commanded all the Jews to leave Rome. And he went to see
them, and because he was of the same trade he stayed with them and
worked.... (Acts 18:1-3)

Paul ... set sail for Syria, and with him Priscilla and Aquila.... And they
came to Ephesus, and he left them there. (Acts 18:18-19)

Now a Jew named Apollos ... came to Ephesus. He was an eloquent man,
competent in the Scriptures. He had been instructed in the way of the Lord.
And being fervent in spirit, he spoke and taught accurately the things con-
cerning Jesus, though he knew only the baptism of John. He began to speak
boldly in the synagogue, but when Priscilla and Aquila heard him, they took
him and explained to him the way of God more accurately. (Acts 18:24-26)

Greet Prisca and Aquila, my fellow workers in Christ Jesus, who risked their necks for my life, to whom not only I give thanks but all the churches of the Gentiles give thanks as well. Greet also the church in their house. (Romans 16:3-5)

The churches of Asia send you greetings. Aquila and Prisca, together with the church in their house, send you hearty greetings in the Lord. (1 Corinthians 16:19)

Despite her transient life, Priscilla made a home wherever she landed. She was a homemaker for her husband, for Paul, and for house churches. She helped her husband instruct Apollos, she risked her neck for Paul, and she sent hearty greetings to other believers because they were her family.

God gave the first family a home, and since their rebellion we all long for a home. Part of the Abrahamic Covenant included people and a place: "On that day the LORD made a covenant with Abram, saying, 'To your offspring I give this land'" (Genesis 15:18). The covenant promise is about family and home: "You shall dwell in the land that I gave to your fathers, and you shall be my people, and I will be your God" (Ezekiel 36:28). The promise was fulfilled in Jesus who dwelt among us and is the way home.

For many women, even Christian women, the longing for a place where they belong causes restlessness and insecurity. But the redeemed woman who has been strengthened in her inner being to know that God has made a place for her in His heart will sing with the psalmist, "Lord, you have been our dwelling place in all generations" (Psalm 90:1). Her soul is secure with Jesus' promise that "if I go and prepare a place for you, I will come again and will take you to myself" (John 14:3). She knows that her "adoption through Jesus Christ" (Ephesians 1:5) makes her part of God's family. She has been rooted and grounded in love; so she rejoices in her historical and global connection to God's children, and she understands that she lives out that connection locally in the church where God has called her to serve. She may not have to risk her neck for her spiritual family, but she is willing to risk her comfort to love her husband and children, to spiritually mother other women, to defend her church family in prayer, to care for and support the weak and the needy and the fearful, to protect the reputation of church leaders by refraining from gossip and criticism, to rescue rebellious women, to comfort the grieving and the lonely. Because God's heart is her home, there is a rootedness that stabilizes her to be a place of grace for those God has chosen to be her family. Other women follow her because her presence is safe and homey. She leads them as she follows Jesus home.

Biblical Foundations for Womanhood resources that amplify concepts in this chapter:
 • Leadership skills for women: *Leadership for Women in the Church.*

NOTES:

1. *Trinity Hymnal* (Atlanta: Great Commission Publications, 1990), #355.
2. *The Holy Bible: English Standard Version* (Wheaton, IL: Crossway Bibles, 2001), footnote, 1199.

Appendix 1

The Danvers Statement –
Rationale and Purposes

RATIONALE

We have been moved in our purpose by the following contemporary developments which we observe with deep concern:

1. The widespread uncertainty and confusion in our culture regarding the complementary differences between masculinity and femininity;

2. the tragic effects of this confusion in unraveling the fabric of marriage woven by God out of the beautiful and diverse strands of manhood and womanhood;

3. the increasing promotion given to feminist egalitarianism with accompanying distortions or neglect of the glad harmony portrayed in Scripture between the loving, humble leadership of redeemed husbands and the intelligent, willing support of that leadership by redeemed wives;

4. the widespread ambivalence regarding the values of motherhood, vocational homemaking, and the many ministries historically performed by women;

5. the growing claims of legitimacy for sexual relationships which have Biblically and historically been considered illicit or perverse, and the increase in pornographic portrayal of human sexuality;

6. the upsurge of physical and emotional abuse in the family;

7. the emergence of roles for men and women in church leadership that do not conform to Biblical teaching but backfire in the crippling of Biblically faithful witness;

8. the increasing prevalence and acceptance of hermeneutical oddities devised to reinterpret apparently plain meanings of Biblical texts;

9. the consequent threat to Biblical authority as the clarity of Scripture is jeopardized and the accessibility of its meaning to ordinary people is withdrawn into the restricted realm of technical ingenuity;

10. and behind all this the apparent accommodation of some within the church to the spirit of the age at the expense of winsome, radical Biblical authenticity which in the power of the Holy Spirit may reform rather than reflect our ailing culture.

PURPOSES

Recognizing our own abiding sinfulness and fallibility, and acknowledging the genuine evangelical standing of many who do not agree with all of our convictions, nevertheless, moved by the preceding observations and by the hope that the noble Biblical vision of sexual complementarity may yet win the mind and heart of Christ's church, we engage to pursue the following purposes:

1. To study and set forth the Biblical view of the relationship between men and women, especially in the home and in the church.

2. To promote the publication of scholarly and popular materials representing this view.

3. To encourage the confidence of lay people to study and understand for themselves the teaching of Scripture, especially on the issue of relationships between men and women.

4. To encourage the considered and sensitive application of this Biblical view in the appropriate spheres of life.

5. And thereby

  —to bring healing to persons and relationships injured by an inadequate grasp of God's will concerning manhood and womanhood,

  —to help both men and women realize their full ministry potential through a true understanding and practice of their God-given roles,

—and to promote the spread of the gospel among all peoples by fostering a Biblical wholeness in relationships that will attract a fractured world.

The "Danvers Statement" was prepared by several evangelical leaders at a meeting of the Council on Biblical Manhood and Womanhood in Danvers, Massachusetts in December 1987. It was first published in final form by the CBMW in Wheaton, Illinois in November 1988. The CBMW grants permission and encourages interested persons to use, reproduce, and distribute the "Danvers Statement." The CBMW can be contacted at 2825 Lexington Road, Box 926, Louisville, Kentucky 40280.

Appendix 2

Titus 2 Discipleship Ministry

*T*his appendix shares an example of a women's ministry that added a Titus 2 discipleship program to their existing Bible studies and service ministries. Three primary factors led the leadership to this decision:

• An awareness of the need to intentionally equip women to understand and live out biblical principles of womanhood in all of life.

• A desire to enfold women who were not involved in a women's Bible study.

• A growing congregation with many women who wanted friendships with other women.

For more information on this ministry, go to www.MidwayPCA.org.

Each church should adapt the following to its own structure and needs.

MIDWAY PRESBYTERIAN CHURCH, POWDER SPRINGS, GEORGIA

WOMEN IN THE CHURCH TITUS 2 DISCIPLESHIP MINISTRY

Purpose and Strategy

The women's ministry submitted the following to the Christian Education Committee, who then submitted it to the elders. *This is included in the Titus 2 training notebook.*

Midway WIC Titus 2 Discipleship Ministry

> You must teach what is in accord with sound doctrine . . . teach the older
> women to be reverent in the way they live, not to be slanderers or addicted
> to much wine, but to teach what is good. Then they can train the younger
> women to love their husbands and children, to be self-controlled and pure,
> to be busy at home, to be kind, and to be subject to their husbands, so that
> no one will malign the word of God. (Titus 2:1, 3-5 [NIV])

Purpose

The purpose of the Women In the Church Titus 2 ministry is to support
the discipleship ministry of the church by helping women establish
covenant relationships with godly women who will encourage and equip
them to live for God's glory.

Goals

• For women to be equipped to apply the principles of biblical womanhood to all of life.

• For women to be equipped to spiritually mother other women and
to show and tell the next generation the biblical principles of womanhood.

• For some women to become Titus 2 group leaders.

• For all participants to be strengthened in their love for and service
to the church.

Foundational Principles for a Titus 2 Discipleship Ministry

Titus 2:3-5 is not simply a suggestion to match older women and
younger women. This directive is a part of covenant life. It is a part of
the strategy for the Christian education of the church.

The Titus mandate was given to the pastor of the church. Paul
instructed Titus to equip older women in the congregation for the ministry of training younger women. This discipleship is to take place
within the context of sound doctrine and under ecclesiastical authority.
The commitment, oversight, and protection of church leadership are biblical and essential.

"Older" women is not just a reference to age. It also involves spiritual maturity. This is a spiritual mothering ministry.

This Titus 2 ministry does not stand alone. It is one component of the women's ministry and of the church's discipleship ministry.

This ministry does not replace existing Bible studies or Circles. Titus groups are informal, small-group topical studies designed to build relationships with godly women and to teach biblical principles of womanhood.

It is important to recognize and celebrate the women who are spontaneously and informally involved in spiritual mothering relationships without participating in this program.

Strategy

1. A Titus 2 committee implements the ministry:
• This committee reports to the WIC Council.
2. Selection of spiritual mothers:
• Names are submitted to the elders for approval and then the committee recruits.
• Women who agree to serve sign the Spiritual Mothering Covenant (below).
• Spiritual mothers report to the Titus 2 committee.
3. Curriculum:
• The *Biblical Foundations for Womanhood* series developed by the Presbyterian Church in America Christian Education and Publications Committee is the curriculum for this ministry.
• These materials are consistent with the doctrinal standards of the church and have been approved by the elders.
• Spiritual mothers agree to use these materials.
4. This is a three-year program:
• The program runs January to January. Rationale: this avoids the "Fall rush" when many church programs begin.
• Women sign up for a year at a time. Rationale: biblical womanhood is countercultural. It requires a massive paradigm shift to think biblically about womanhood and to live covenantally as a woman. The first year emphasizes building relationships. In year two, it is expected that women will begin to make the paradigm shift in their thinking about womanhood. Year three emphasizes the application of the principles of womanhood to life and relationships.

• By the end of this cycle it is anticipated that women will be equipped to fulfill the goals of the ministry.

• Year 1: *Spiritual Mothering* (if a group completes this study they may also use *The True Woman*).

• Year 2: *By Design* (if a group completes this study they may also use *Treasures of Encouragement*).

• Year 3: *The Legacy of Biblical Womanhood.*

5. Assignment to groups:

• Each spiritual mother decides the time her group will meet. There are morning, afternoon and night groups. There are some Wednesday night groups that meet at the church since there is child-care at that time.

• The times of the gatherings are publicized and women sign up for a time that is convenient for them. The names of the leaders are not given. Rationale: this is not a personality-driven ministry. The publicity explains that unity in Christ is not determined by common interests or circumstances.

6. Groups:

• Groups meet monthly so that this ministry does not compete with other aspects of church life.

• Groups have six to eight women.

• It is suggested that groups meet in the leader's home, and/or in homes of participants.

• Groups determine whether or not they will vary their schedule in the summer.

• Women who sign up for the second or third year normally remain with their same group. However, if they have a scheduling conflict they may switch to a more convenient time.

7. Training the spiritual mothers:

• The committee is responsible for training.

• Leaders study *The Legacy of Biblical Womanhood* and the book they will use that year. They are encouraged to read all of the *Biblical Foundations for Womanhood* books.

• The following materials are in the training notebook and are covered in training sessions:

Purpose and Strategy

Spiritual Mothering Covenant (see below)
Guidelines for Titus 2 Leaders (see below)
Biblical Principles of Womanhood (see page 35 of this book)

8. The vision and purpose of the ministry is maintained through:

• A yearly gathering for the combined groups. Testimonies and ideas are shared.

• Two or three gatherings for spiritual mothers throughout the year to share successes and concerns, to pray together, and to give additional instruction and encouragement.

• Testimonies from spiritual mothers and/or daughters at women's ministry events.

9. Teen girls: The Titus 2 committee works with the Youth Ministry to help teen girls establish relationships with Midway women and to begin introducing them to the concepts of biblical womanhood. There are a variety of opportunities for teen girls such as:

• An occasional Sunday school class for high school girls to teach biblical womanhood.

• A summer seminar on biblical womanhood for middle school girls.

• Three or four gatherings each year for high school girls in homes of Midway women. Each woman who hosts the girls tells them about herself and her family through family pictures, stories of a special piece of furniture or dishes, favorite books. She tells about her faith by sharing her testimony, or by telling the girls about women who influenced her life, or how she started attending the church. The hostess plans an activity or craft to teach a skill such as flower arranging, napkin folding, cross-stitching, cake decorating. She does this herself or asks another woman to take this responsibility. She also provides refreshments. At each gathering, a Titus 2 leader gives a brief devotion based on a principle of biblical womanhood. Sometimes the craft/skill coordinates with the devotion. For example:

A devotion on hospitality/demonstrate table setting.

A devotion on encouragement/teach the girls to write notes of encouragement. Have note cards available and let the girls spend time writing a note to someone.

Summary of the Process

Step 1: The Women In the Church Council spent several months praying and evaluating the need.

Step 2: The WIC Council submitted a request to the Christian Education Committee to explore beginning a Titus 2 Ministry. This was discussed and then given to the elders for approval.

Step 3: The WIC Council developed the purpose and strategy. This was submitted to the Christian Education Committee and approved by the elders.

Step 4: Throughout the process newsletter articles educated and informed the congregation of the purpose and plan for this ministry.

Step 5: Implementation:

• July - August: a list of potential spiritual mothers is submitted to the elders for approval, then the committee recruits leaders.

• September - December: spiritual mothers are trained.

• Mid-November - December: women sign up to participate. There is a large sign-up board with the times for each group listed. After sign-up, the Titus 2 leader calls the women in her group. The women also receive a letter from the committee inviting them to a gathering for the combined groups.

• January: all of the groups meet together at the church. The purpose, goals and procedures are explained. Groups sit together at tables hosted by the spiritual mothers. Each spiritual mother brings items from her home to use as her centerpiece and to introduce herself to her group (family pictures, examples of hobbies, favorite books). She asks a woman in the group to bring items to the next meeting that will help the group get to know her better. Books are distributed and the leaders explain the importance of everyone reading the assigned chapter and coming prepared to discuss it.

• June: the committee meets with the spiritual mothers to evaluate and to see if they will serve another year.

Spiritual Mothering Covenant

This is included in the training notebook.

You must teach what is in accord with sound doctrine . . . teach the older women to be reverent in the way they live, not to be slanderers or addicted to much wine, but to teach what is good. Then they can train the younger women to love their husbands and children, to be self-controlled and pure, to be busy at home, to be kind, and to be subject to their husbands, so that no one will malign the word of God. (Titus 2:1, 3-5) [NIV]

_____I am a member of Midway church.

_____I am in agreement with the doctrinal standards of the church (*The Westminster Confession of Faith and the Larger and Shorter Catechisms.*)

_____As a spiritual mother I will support the work of the church, defend the unity of the church, and submit to the elders of the church.

_____I agree to use the materials that have been approved by the elders.

_____ (If married): My husband is supportive of my participation in this ministry.

_____If a woman confides in me about serious problems, I understand that I am not to assume the role of a counselor. I should encourage her to contact the pastor or an elder, and if appropriate offer to do this for her.

Signed: _____

Guidelines for Titus 2 Leaders

This is included in the training notebook.

1. Verses to guide leaders:

• Galatians 4:19 My little children, for whom I am again in the anguish of childbirth until Christ is formed in you!

• 1 Thessalonians 2:7-8 But we were gentle among you, like a nursing mother taking care of her own children. So, being affectionately desirous of you, we were ready to share with you not only the gospel of God but also our own selves, because you had become very dear to us.

2. At your first gathering share personal and group parameters. This will help prevent unrealistic expectations of the leader and inherent dangers in small groups. For example:

• Tell women if there are times when it is not convenient for them to call you.

• If you are meeting in your home, set the time limits and explain if they need to leave by a certain time.

• There is to be no gossip or dishonoring another person. Explain that if at any time you feel that discussions are becoming critical of others, it is part of your mothering ministry to tell them and to redirect the conversation.

• Explain that if they are dealing with a difficult relationship, your responsibility is to help them reclaim the relationship for God's glory by reflecting God's grace into that relationship. We often cannot change our circumstances, and we cannot change another person, but we can pray for God to change us so that we reflect His grace.

3. You are not to teach a lesson. You are to facilitate a discussion based on an assigned chapter of the book.

• Ask women to be prepared to share one or two insights or questions from each chapter.

• You may want to use the questions at the end of the chapter as discussion points and/or prepare questions to direct the discussion.

• It may take several times to find the right approach for your group. Some groups are fine with simply sharing insights while others need to be more guided.

• Pray, laugh, and spend time building relationships.

4. It may take several gatherings for the women to become comfortable with one another. Be intentional in helping them develop relationships. Suggestions:

• Pray for an atmosphere of love and encouragement.

• Pray together. Share prayer requests and items of praise. You may want to keep a prayer journal. Encourage women to select specific Scriptures to pray for one another and for situations.

• Each time you meet pray for the church. You may want to pray for a specific ministry in the church, or a missionary, or a pastor and his family. You may want to send them a card of encouragement.

• At each gathering ask someone to be prepared to share about herself, or ask everyone to bring a wedding picture, or a favorite vacation picture, or something that shows a special interest/hobby.

• Ask women to be prepared to share a testimony, or a favorite Scripture verse or hymn, or a childhood memory.

• Plan a "sharing a skill day" when someone teaches a craft or skill, or have lunch together, or plan a gathering for the families.

• Plan a ministry to do together: visit a nursing home, take a meal to someone.

5. Caution: groups should not become inward-focused.

• The church should be blessed because of this ministry.

• This ministry should build unity in the church.

• The group should pray for the church and the leaders.

• The group should intentionally consider ways to minister to and enfold others.

6. Relationship discussions:

• Use *The Legacy of Biblical Womanhood*, Part 2, to guide discussions about relationships. Teach the women to identify the relationship and the governing principle.

7. Who talks?

• Monitor how much you talk. You are guiding a discussion, not teaching a lesson.

• If one or two women dominate discussions, ask specific women to share their thoughts about the topic, or ask that everyone share an insight.

• Be careful not to promote personal agendas.

• Be slow to give solutions. Encourage women to go to God's Word to determine how to think biblically and live covenantally. Explain that you will not always have an answer to their questions and problems, but your desire is to help them keep their eyes upon the Lord.

8. Crisis Situations:

• Spiritual mothers should not assume the role of a counselor.

• If there is a crisis situation, or serious problems such as drugs or abuse, a spiritual mother should not try to handle this alone. She should help the woman to think and act biblically.

• A spiritual mother may offer to go with her to the appropriate person (pastor or elder).

• If a spiritual mother is not sure what advice is appropriate, she should tell the spiritual daughter that she does not know and inform her that she will ask for assistance from the pastor or an elder.

Concluding Observations from the Titus 2 Committee

Many of our Titus 2 leaders do not consider themselves to be teachers, but they are mothers in Israel who have a passion to guide other women to spiritual maturity.

We did not know what to expect when the program was introduced. We prayed and planned for seven groups. They were all filled and we had to add a group. By the second year, many women who were only involved in Sunday morning worship began participating. The Titus groups have become a significant entry-point to community life.

The variety of women who participate is thrilling. There are stay-at-home moms, homeschooling moms, professional women, single women, college women and empty-nesters. The Lord's blessing on this ministry has been beyond anything we ever dreamed or imagined. We are grateful to Him for allowing us to be a part of what He is doing in our church.

Appendix 3

Women's Bible Studies

*T*he following articles give helpful information for selecting curricula for women's Bible studies.

EVALUATING BIBLE STUDY MATERIALS

LINDA SMOOKLER
GLASGOW REFORMED PRESBYTERIAN CHURCH,
GLASGOW, DELAWARE

(This is used by permission. It is excerpted from "Thinking Biblically— Evaluating Women's Bible Study Materials," an article first published in the Treasures of Encouragement *e-magazine: www.treasuresofencouragement.org)*

In evaluating Bible study materials, we must remember that women are daily assaulted with the perversions of the world, the flesh, and the devil. It is a daily challenge to think biblically. We think biblically when, no matter what the world says, our thoughts are shaped by Scripture. We think biblically when we evaluate everything by the Word of God alone. We think biblically when God's Word is our authority.

James 3:1 is compelling: "Not many of you should become teachers, my brothers, for you know that we who teach will be judged with greater strictness."

When a teacher stands before women and says, "Thus says the Lord," she must be sure that she is conveying truth. The church is to be "the pillar and support" of the truth. Our first concern is to give teachers materials that teach biblical truth.

In our church, before we evaluate curricula for our women's Bible studies, we consider our long-term and short-term goals. Our women's ministry purpose statement directs the goals for everything we do. We often have a yearly theme, and if possible we coordinate with a sermon series or a Sunday school focus. Bible studies should be purposeful, so we select material that will help us accomplish our goals.

When we preview and evaluate curricula, we make the following observations:

1. Is Scripture the authority?

How much Scripture does each chapter contain? The best books are full of Scriptural quotations and are built around Scriptural principles. Scripture is used to explain and support Scripture in a clear pattern of building precept upon precept. Contrast that with books that give a hypothesis and then pull one or two Scripture quotations out of context to support their premise.

Is Scripture put on the same level as experience? Is the Bible the only authority or is a person's theory or opinion treated as equally valuable with Scripture? Is experience evaluated by Scripture or is Scripture subjected to varying interpretations and experiences?

2. What is the doctrinal perspective?

Does the book compromise the essentials of the faith: creation, the fall of man, the virgin birth, the sinless life of Christ, the atonement, a physical resurrection? Does it violate any of the *solas*: Scripture alone, grace alone, through faith alone, in Christ alone, for the glory of God alone?

3. Does it teach salvation by grace through faith?

Does the book compromise on or support the need for repentance, reconciliation and reliance? Does it confront the sin nature, focus on our fundamental need for reconciliation and our responsibility to be a witness to a lost world? Does it make clear the reality of the necessity of total reliance on grace as a lifestyle? Does it emphasize the use of the means of grace (worship, prayer, the Word, fellowship, communion, meditating, memorizing)?

4. Who is the author?

What do we know about the author? What is their background or reputation? What else have they written? Would use of this book give an endorsement to all of their books? How does the author view women and women's role in the church?

5. Who does the author quote?

It is important to know who the author reads. Do they quote the Puritans, the classics, familiar trusted theologians?

6. Is the book God-centered or man-centered?

Is the emphasis how we can be conformed to the image of God and glorify God or how we can be satisfied and happy?

7. Is the book teachable and useful?

Can it be easily taught by our leaders? Can our leaders determine and communicate the central truth of each chapter? Does the book delve into issues that our leaders are not prepared to address? Is the subject matter of each chapter appropriate for our use? Is there a workbook or can lesson plans be easily developed from the chapters? What will the book equip our women to know and do?

It is hard to find a perfect book, but if there are more than a few questions it is best not to use it. If a book needs a lot of explaining, what will happen to the woman who comes once or twice and doesn't return? We don't want to put something into her hands that will confuse her.

We use topical books because they systematize what the Bible says on a particular subject and they give careful explanations, illustrations and applications. In order to promote unity and intimacy among the women, we often have everyone study the same book, usually a *Biblical Foundations for Womanhood* book, during the Fall semester. Then we offer several selections in the Spring. We want to equip women to fulfill their various callings, particularly their calling as women in the church, and we want to fulfill our calling to be Titus 2 women to them.

PLANNING, CHOOSING, AND EVALUATING BIBLE STUDIES

DONNA DOBBS

FIRST PRESBYTERIAN CHURCH, JACKSON, MISSISSIPPI

I've been a Christian Education Director for twenty-three years, and whenever educators get together the first thing they want to know is what curricula you use. After years of searching, I have good news and bad news. The bad news is that I have not found that magic curricula. The good news is that I have learned what questions to ask when looking for a good study.

How do we decide what we need to study?

1. Evaluate

Begin the evaluation process by determining what is needed. Do not choose a study based on the popularity of a writer, filling up space in a program, or the demands of consumers. People tend to get excited about personalities or cultural trends, but these are not good reasons to choose a study. Those making decisions about what a group should study should pray for God's wisdom to discern the real needs of women. People's felt needs must always be compared with God's demands and our responsibilities before Him. There are genuine needs, but these must be seen in relation to biblical values. Ask questions such as:

• What are the biblical and theological basics that our church considers to be essential?

• What areas of knowledge, understanding, values, attitudes, and skills within the group can we identify?

• What is the level of biblical knowledge? Do the women need information? Do they have a foundation of Bible knowledge? Is there an area that has not been taught and is needed? Do they need gospel or growth—milk or meat?

• What areas of the Christian life need to be addressed?

• What is the lifestage of the group? Are there a variety of ages or is the group homogenous? This usually affects expectations of study time, overall commitment, and sometimes the topic.

• How spiritually mature is the group? How much individual study will they do? How well do they know each other? Are they all church members?

2. Coordinate with other teaching ministries

• Would it be beneficial for several groups to study themes that complement one another? Are there ways the study could support the preaching topics, Sunday school studies, and other Bible studies in the church?

3. Determine goals

• Based on the evaluation, determine specific goals for the study.

What should we study?

The kind of study you select should be determined by the goals. What will help you accomplish these goals?

• A specific topic. This is harder to teach and places huge demands on the teacher unless you have a curriculum that addresses this particular topic.

• A book: Be careful not to follow the latest trend or popular author. Most teachers find books difficult to teach unless there is a Teacher's Guide with lesson plans and/or a student workbook.

• A book of the Bible: This should always be the backbone of your curricula. Resourcing and training are essential to develop good teachers.

• Videos: There are a number of reasons that videos are inferior to real live teachers, and most of the time when I opt to use one I realize that it's because I have failed to do my job in giving a vision to people about personal ministry and in training them to minister. Occasionally we use videos, but it's not my first choice. They can provide good information and professional presentations, and that can be very alluring, but video studies are inferior because nothing can take the place of the "redeemed personality" in the classroom. That person may not have a seminary level education, but she is called and gifted by God to serve His church and His people. She knows her audience, loves her students, intercedes for them before God's throne, and gives her personal time to encourage and counsel those in her class. No video study can equal those benefits in the life of another person.

How do we evaluate materials?

Some of the primary considerations in evaluating materials are:

• Use of Scripture: What is the view of Scripture? What is the place of Scripture? Is Scripture the starting point or does it take a psychological or behavioral approach? What provision is made for the use of the

Bible by the student? Will students need to study the Word? Does it use Scripture correctly or does it simply baptize an idea with a verse out of context? Is the curricula primarily experienced-centered or God-centered? Does it take an individualistic approach to Christian life and growth or does it reflect a covenantal approach to faith and life?

• Theology: What does this book teach about the Triune God—Father, Son, Holy Spirit—man, sin, salvation, Christian growth, the local church?

• Doctrine: What doctrines are emphasized? Which doctrines are not included? What is the basic approach to biblical interpretation? Are there any areas of distortion? Is it doctrinally consistent with the standards of the church?

Spiritual Mothering, by Susan Hunt
Challenges women to put Titus
2 into action, mentoring younger
women in the church.
0-89107-719-7, $13.99

**The Legacy of Biblical
Womanhood**, by Susan Hunt &
Barbara Thompson
Equips women to think biblically, live
covenantally, and pass the legacy
of biblical womanhood to the next
generation.
1-58134-454-6, $12.99

By Design, by Susan Hunt
Helps women understand God's
"helper" design for them, and
rallies the church to fully utilize the
resources of its women.
0-89107-976-9, $12.99

The True Woman, by Susan Hunt
Exhorts and instructs women in
making an impact for eternity by
way of their God-given purpose.
0-89107-927-0, $12.99

**A Leader's Guide for this book is included in
Women's Mir~~istry: A Training and Resour~~ce Guide**